First
Choices

First Choices

Teaching children aged 4 to 8 to make positive decisions about their own lives

Margaret Collins

P·C·P
Paul Chapman
Publishing

Paul Chapman Publishing
A SAGE Publications Company
1 Oliver's Yard
55 City Road
London EC1Y 1SP

SAGE Publications Inc.
2455 Teller Road
Thousand Oaks, California 91320

SAGE Publications India Pvt Ltd.
B-42, Panchsheel Enclave
Post Box 4109
New Delhi 110 017

Commissioning Editors: Barbara Maines and George Robinson
Editorial Team: Mel Maines, Sarah Lynch, Wendy Ogden.
Designer: Nick Shearn
Illustrator: Mark Ruffle

A catalogue record for this book is available from the British Library

Library of Congress Control Number 2005907009

ISBN10 1-4129-1310-1
ISBN13 978-1-4129-1310-2
ISBN10 1-4129-1305-5 (pbk)
ISBN13 978-1-4129-1305-8 (pbk)

Printed on paper from sustainable resources

Printed in Great Britain by The Cromwell Press Ltd, Trowbridge, Wiltshire

Contents

How to use the CD-ROM

The CD-ROM contains PDF files, labelled 'Colour illustrations.pdf' and 'Line illustrations.pdf' which consist of posters and drawings to colour in for each lesson in this resource. You will need Acrobat Reader version 3 or higher to view and print these resources.

The documents are set up to print to A4 but you can enlarge them to A3 by increasing the output percentage at the point of printing using the page set-up settings for your printer.

Preface

Making choices is central to the human condition. From the moment we become conscious human beings we can choose how we respond and with whom we interact in the social world. The ability to choose increases through time. The individual's self-awareness, self-esteem, locus of control (that is, the ability to gain internal control) all impact upon these choices and the ways in which they are made.

The stories in this series are based around the problems and joys of living as a child and young person within the twenty first century. They highlight the essential choices that people have to make in order to survive and function in a world that can seem complex and, at times, difficult to understand.

This series consists of three books which aim to help children and young people to make the kinds of choices that will achieve the best possible outcomes. There is consequently a focus throughout on the ways in which both feelings and the brain inform behaviour and our capacity to influence and make good life choices. The intention is to encourage the listener to become aware of the differences between thinking, feeling and behaving and the ways in which they can distinguish between responses based on thoughts or feelings and the majority of responses which are based on both. The aim is to encourage them to distinguish between impulsive or well thought out responses which allow for good and positive outcomes.

The series provides a 'safe' medium, the story, in which children can both identify and reflect upon good and negative choices and the outcomes that will ensue from both. Each book is designed to target a specific age range from early years to late adolescence. There are themes that are common to all three books. These include issues such as inclusion, peer pressure, grief, loss, separation and coping with change among others which are pertinent to young people's lives and experiences.

Each book contains a series of stories which include opportunities for discussion, reflection and a range of follow on and reinforcement activities. There is a focus throughout on creativity and problem-solving which can be undertaken within a climate of empathy, tolerance and mutual support. The stories in the series would fulfil many of the PSHE/Citizenship requirements. Although the primary aim of the stories is to help children to make good choices and to become good citizens, we would emphasise the importance of the stories themselves. They are not merely didactic tools. They are meant to be read or listened to and enjoyed in their own right.

Margaret Collins, Tina Rae and Phil Carradice

Introduction and Background

If we can help children to understand that both their feelings and their brain inform their behaviours they can begin to develop the ability to make good choices. This book introduces choice strategies to present to children as a range of options. The aim is to encourage children to become aware of the differences between thinking, feeling and behaving; the ways in which they can use both the brain and feelings in order to inform behaviour. We need to help them to distinguish between responses that are based upon only thoughts or only feelings and begin to realise that better responses are normally based upon both.

This will also enable children to distinguish between impulsive and well thought out reactions and behaviours; those which will result in good choices and gain them the best possible outcomes.

This programme provides children with opportunities to understand these distinctions within a 'safe' medium, i.e. the story, in which they have the opportunity to identify and reflect upon good choices and outcomes that they may or may not make.

Locus of control

Key to this process is the concept of locus of control. The stories in the programme show children reacting to certain situations with both internal and external control. Internal control is when you are, or feel that you are, in control or responsible for your own behaviours and responses. External control is when you feel that you are being controlled or that your behaviours are the direct result of someone else's behaviour in the situation in which you find yourself.

There is a strong emphasis on the need to develop internal control in order to make good choices and to develop and sustain positive behaviour. Acceptance of the consequences of one's own behaviours and the importance of understanding how one's own feelings and thoughts impact upon them are also key.

Emotional literacy and mental health

The stories in this programme show characters dealing with a range of problems and dilemmas in which they have to make choices about the ways in which they respond. These choices frequently depend upon their ability to engage with both their brain and their feelings in order to decide what to do.

There is, throughout each story, a focus on encouraging children to reflect upon their own feelings and behaviours and also to recognise, label and cope with the range of feelings that they will experience on a daily basis in everyday life both in school and in the wider community.

Research links children's mental health and physical health to the development of emotional literacy (Goleman 1995, Grant 1992, Rudd 1998). Peter Sharp (2001) suggests four main reasons why emotional literacy must be promoted in both children and adults. He states that we need to:

1) recognise our emotions in order to be able to label and define them

2) understand our emotions in order to become effective learners

3) handle and manage our emotions in order to be able to develop and sustain positive relationships

4) appropriately express emotions in order to develop as rounded people who are able to help ourselves and, in turn, those around us.

The latter reason also implies that, in order to help ourselves and consequently make 'good' choices, we need to develop internal control alongside the ability to use both brain and feelings to make a choice. This means recognising and preventing impulsive responses when they are not helpful, using instead our ability to think ahead. If we use our brain to identify consequences of actions we stand a good chance of making a good choice and achieving the best possible outcome.

As Rae, Marris and Koeries (2005) state:

'Building emotional literacy and providing children with daily opportunities to develop their skills in this area will also simultaneously help to promote good mental health and nurture children's ability to be resilient and to cope with the challenges that life may bring them.' (p.27)

Challenges and pressures

Coping with challenges and pressures is, of course, a reality of everyday life for children and it is therefore essential that we help them to develop the emotional resilience and ability to engage the brain and feelings to inform behaviours and make choices that will ensure positive outcomes. The challenges and pressures are many and varied. In this programme the following have been highlighted. Coping with:

▸ environment

▸ stealing

- lying
- social behaviours
- justice
- loss, grief, separation
- prejudice
- disability
- risk.

Within these areas, the listening children will be required to make choices about the way in which they think the story characters (and, by implication, they themselves) would respond and behave. It is hoped that this programme will provide the children with the opportunities to develop the skills and self-awareness needed to make good life choices which are positive for themselves and those with whom they live and work.

Age range of this book

The programme in this book specifically aims to help children in Reception to Year 4 to develop the ability to make good choices and to make use of both brain and feelings to inform behaviours which will achieve them the best possible outcomes. The first story in each pair is more suited to the younger children, the second for older children. Teachers of children with special needs will find this programme useful for one to one or small group teaching.

Aims of the programme

The aims of the programme are as follows:

- to enable children to understand how thoughts, feelings and behaviours are related
- to encourage children to develop self-control and internal control
- to enable children to develop self-talk and self-reflection strategies in order to modify and inform behaviours
- to recognise impulsive responses and learn to use the brain in order to inhibit these
- to develop empathy and more awareness of others' intentions
- to be able to more accurately predict their own behaviours and to identify the consequences of their behaviours

- to help children to identify solutions and good choices via small or intermediate steps as opposed to simply emphasising ends or goals to encourage children to generate a range of alternative solutions
- to enable children to identify the feelings that they experience and to gain a deeper understanding of them
- to further develop self-knowledge, self-esteem and self-worth
- to affirm the validity of others' positions and feelings and to respect and accept differences in order to promote a sense of equality
- to help children to develop problem-solving skills within a supportive group context, recognising how they can learn from each other's experience
- to encourage children to identify problems as challenges which can be met by their own resources, skills and support systems.

Structure of the Programme

There are nine themes, each with two stories. The first story is more appropriate for younger children and the second for older children. You may wish to use both stories and activities or to choose the one most appropriate for the age and stage of the children in your class.

The structure of each theme

Each section is structured as follows:

Focus

The main focus points are highlighted prior to a brief summary of the story. These can be used to inform you or as part of an introduction for the children in the group. You may wish to record the focus points on the board before the start of the session.

The story and Flag points

As you read the story to the children you will see Flag points within the text which pick up on key themes or raise particular points of interest with the children. You can choose whether to stop at each point or read the story straight through to the end before using Flag points for discussion or questions before starting the activities. The Flag points are not intended as any kind of straitjacket and you may wish to tailor these to the interests or needs of the class.

Activities

The activities are provided in order to further clarify or build on key concepts, themes or choices encountered in the story.

The first activity takes the form of a Circle Time discussion about the story, the characters and the choice they have to make. Teachers who already use Circle Time for discussion and involvement will already have rules in place. Teachers who do not yet use Circle Time can find information about setting up and running successful Circle Time sessions in books such as *Circle Time for the Very Young* (Collins, M. 2001).

The first activity is followed by further tasks which you may like the children to undertake. You may not want your children to do all the activities; select those appropriate for the children in your class. You may prefer to do some of the activities in another session.

Homework

This activity is intended to be undertaken outside the school context and will usually require children to involve their families or other people in gathering information and investigating views and available resources.

Reflection

This draws the children back into the story and highlights the kinds of choices they themselves might have to make in circumstances similar to those of the characters in the story. The emphasis is on stopping and thinking, with their head as well as with their feelings, when they themselves have to make choices.

Two endings

Each story is provided with two endings, both of which should be read to the children after they have completed the activities. While these endings are not necessarily 'good' and 'bad' they will aid further reflection about the characters' needs to accept the consequences of their actions.

The focus here is on identifying the choices made and whether or not these were the best or most informed choices, by incorporating both brain and feelings to inform behaviour. Ask the children to discuss these endings and to say which would achieve the best possible outcome for the characters involved. Give them the opportunity to suggest alternative endings for you all to talk about, draw or write about.

Setting up the programme

The sessions in this programme are set out in a structured way but you may wish to adapt them according to the responses and interests of the children. The story, activities and reflection approach allows for such flexibility and encourages children to pursue ideas and themes of particular interest at any point in the session. However, for convenience and ease of use, the framework is a clear route towards achieving the central objectives.

It may be helpful for the teacher to take note of the following points when setting up the activities.

Size of group

This programme is designed to be delivered to whole classes but can also easily be adapted for smaller groups of children. However you arrange your group, it is important to ensure that all children can participate and reflect within the session. Adequate talking time is essential if children are really to benefit from the content and begin to develop new skills.

Setting the tone

It is essential to set the tone for these sessions right at the start of the programme and to emphasise the way in which all views and contributions will be listened to and valued. As a key aim of the programme is to help children to understand and make 'good' choices, it is vital that the climate of the group is both supportive and nurturing from the outset. A good structure is to use your Circle Time arrangements, with agreed rules, as a platform for the story, discussions and activities wherever possible.

Using the stories and activities

The stories are designed to improve children's problem-solving skills, self-reflection and self-awareness.

The Flag points are intended to pick out key themes and ideas and to prompt the above processes. It is vital to ensure adequate discussion time. It is for you to decide how these Flag points are covered. For some, it may seem more comfortable and logical to stop at each marked stage in the story while for others it may be more practical to read the story without stopping and then pose the questions afterwards. This may to some extent depend upon the age, concentration and memory levels of the children.

Each story ends abruptly when one or more of the characters is faced with having to make a choice. It is hoped that this 'cliff-hanger' will provoke the children into making many and varied suggestions as to these choices.

You will know which activities are the most appropriate for your children. It may happen that you or the children develop an entirely different and new activity as a result of the story and question process. Ultimately, this is a flexible framework; what is important is that the children's interests and ideas are given space for development.

The given endings

It is important to emphasise that none of the given endings are the 'right' endings. There may be advantages and disadvantages in some of them and the most important thing is for children to be able to analyse the choices, decisions and actions taken by the individual characters in the stories. Once again, allocating adequate time for this purpose is essential as is ensuring an open forum for debate via your Circle Time process.

Parental involvement

It is important to approach work outside school with sensitivity. You may find it helpful to provide and send home a brief outline of the programme and its key objectives. In this, you could give a brief description of the approaches adopted and the way that children are being encouraged to utilise both brain and feelings in order to inform the decision-making process. In this way you will be able to enlist the interest and cooperation of parents or carers so that they understand the nature of the programme, the ways in which it aims to help children to develop problem-solving and self-reflection skills in order to identify and make good choices.

Using the CD

All the stories, without the Flag points, are reproduced on the CD together with the pictures in colour. You could use the pictures as part of a display of work relating to the story, adding excerpts of the story. You may like to print some of the stories, with the picture printed on card as a cover, for the children to read or to put in your class or school library. You could help the children to make individual books by printing the colour picture as a cover and adding a blank sheet at the end for children to write their own ending before taking their book home to share with their families.

Forward thinking

It is hoped that this programme will be an enjoyable learning experience for both you and the children and that the links they will make between the affective and cognitive domains will continue to inform their future choices and decision-making. To achieve this, consider how you can include the making of emotionally literate choices through and beyond the taught curriculum.

This programme needs to be viewed as a prompt to this wider process of providing all children with both the forum and the skills needed to make good life choices – ones which will ensure the mental well-being and safety of both themselves and those in their families and communities.

Bibliography

Collins, M. (2001) *Circle Time for the Very Young*, London, Paul Chapman Publishing, SAGE.

Koeries, J., Marris, B. & Rae, T. (2005) *Problem Postcards Social, Emotional and Behavioural Skills Training for Disaffected and Difficult Children aged 7 to 11*, Bristol, Lucky Duck Publishing.

Goleman, D. (1995) *Emotional Intelligence – Why it Matters More than IQ*, London, Bloomsbury.

Grant, W.T. (1992) *Consortium on the School Based Promotion of Social Competence, Drugs and Alcohol Prevention Curricula*, San Francisco, Josey-Bass.

Rudd, B. (1998) *Talking is for Kids*, Bristol, Lucky Duck Publishing.

Sharp, P. (2001) *Nurturing Emotional Literacy: A Practical Guide for Teachers, Parents and those in the Caring Professions*, London, David Fulton Publishers.

Gourley, P. (1999) *Teaching Self-control in the Classroom – A Cognitive Behavioural Approach*, Bristol, Lucky Duck Publishing.

The Stories and Activities

Section 1: Environment

Story 1: Playing in the Park

Focus

- ▶ the need to protect one's self when making decisions

- ▶ care for wildlife

- ▶ environmental protection

- ▶ use head and feelings before making decisions.

This story is about two five year olds playing in the park and coming across broken glass. The immediate decision of one child is to pick up the glass but is this the right thing to do? Secondary issues are about keeping safe in the sun and taking litter home.

Either stop the story and discuss the Flag points as you read or read the story straight through and use these as discussion points before doing the activities.

Jenny and Ian didn't live near each other but they had met at playschool when they started there at three years old. From that day they had been buddies and now they had started school they were in the same class. Sometimes they joined groups of other children when they played outside but a lot of the time they played as a twosome. Their parents had got to know each other and sometimes Jenny went to Ian's house to play and sometimes Ian went to Jenny's.

One very sunny day in the summer holidays, when they were both playing at Jenny's house, her mother asked them if they would like to go to the play park. They liked going there because there were not only swings and slides and other things to play on but there was a pool where you could paddle or sail boats as well as gardens and places to sit and have picnics. So when Jenny's mum asked if they would like to go there for a picnic, they both yelled, 'Yes please!' Ian looked sad for a moment and then said, 'But I haven't got my swim trunks, so I can't go in the water!' Jenny's mum was ready for that and said, 'Well, we'll just have to go that way round and collect them from your house on the way, I'll give your mum a ring to make sure she's in.'

While Jenny's mum made a picnic, the children put a towel, sun lotion and

Jenny's boats into a bag as well as her swimming gear and soon they were ready to set off. Jenny had her sun hat on, but Ian's was at home, so because it was very hot in the sun, they walked on the shady side of the streets.

Flag: Do the children know about the danger of too much sun and the ways to keep safe when it is very sunny? Do they know that hats, sun lotion, clothes to protect and sunshades will keep their skin safe? Do they know that it is good to drink water to stop dehydration?

When they got to Ian's house his mum was waiting at the gate with his swimming trunks and sun hat. Now they both wore hats with brims on and Jenny's mum had her hat and sunglasses on, so they walked in the sun until they got to the park.

First they went to look at the pond and saw that several other families were picnicking there. They put their swimming things on and went into the water. They had a good time, splashing around and sailing Jenny's two boats. After a little while the two children wanted something to eat, so Jenny's mum got out the picnic and they all sat down on the grass and ate sandwiches and fruit. Then they drank some of the water.

When they had all had enough to eat and drink, Ian said, 'Let's go to the play park now, I want to go on the big slide,' so they packed up their picnic, carefully putting all the papers and left over food in the bag and started off towards the play area.

Flag: Do your children take their rubbish home or do they leave a mess? Can they think of any danger if they put it into a rubbish bin? Do they know that there could be unsafe things inside rubbish bins that cut or hurt them?

Around the play park there were seats so Jenny's mum found a shady one and settled down. She had a book to read, but kept on looking up to make sure the children were safe and happy. She knew that the play apparatus was safe because there was a special green surface underneath to stop people getting hurt if they fell. There were about a dozen other children of all ages playing; some of these children were really too big to be playing on these young children's apparatus. She watched as Ian and Jenny ran off to the big slide. However, as the children walked around the slide towards the steps, Ian noticed the sun glinting on something and saw that there was a lot of broken glass on the ground. 'Wait a minute,' he said, as he bent down to look at the glass. 'Someone's broken a bottle here and this is dangerous,' he said. 'People could get hurt if they fell on it; think of the dogs and other creatures that could hurt their paws if they walked on this. We must pick it all up,' Ian decided and bent down to start to pick up the jagged pieces of glass…

Activities

After reading the story, ask the children to think about whether Ian is doing the safe thing in picking up the glass. Ask children to touch their elbows if they think Ian is doing the right thing and to touch their nose, if they can think of something better to do. Count up the numbers and note this down.

Ask volunteers who can think of a better thing to do to finish the sentence: 'I think Ian could…' or 'I think Jenny could…'. Make a list of what the children say.

They could:

- kick the glass away with their feet
- get some paper to use to protect them as they pick up the glass
- tell Jenny's mum
- tell the park-keeper
- play on the swings instead
- ignore the glass and go on the slide anyway
- tell older children.

Read through the list with the children and talk about these decisions that the children could have made. Ask them which decisions were made using their feelings and which they made using their heads. Put a red ring around those that the children think were decisions made using their feelings and a blue ring around those made using their heads. How many rings in each colour? Are they all blue?

Look again at the list and ask your class to decide which are the best decisions for the children to make. Number your decision list and ask the children to vote with their feet to show which decision they think is the best one. ('Vote with your feet' is when the children move to a certain place in the classroom according to their choice of decision and stand in a group.) Ask each group to count themselves in and put these numbers alongside your written list.

Ask the children to consider the implications of broken glass in the play park. Ask them to tell you what could happen to people and wildlife if it is left there for a long time.

Ask the children to think about and tell you what could happen if the broken glass had been near or in the paddling pool.

Talk about what could happen if the children had left all their picnic leftovers on the grass near where they had their picnic. Suppose everyone always left their picnic rubbish there?

Talk about what could happen if they put their hands into a refuse bag – what unsafe things could be inside?

Ask the children to work in groups of four or five to work out a good ending to this story. Ask them to role-play their ending, after first deciding who will be the children, the adults or bystanders. Come together in the circle and ask volunteers to show their ending.

Ask the children to draw or write about their ending and make a display of this work alongside a brief resume of the story. Use large speech bubbles with statements or questions to make the display interactive. You could add this work to other work on protecting the environment or work about keeping safe.

Homework

Ask the children to tell their families about this work and ask them if they can suggest any good decisions to make if they find broken glass in a place where children play. Ask them to bring back their families' suggestions to the next Circle Time.

Reflection

Remind them of the Flag points in the story.

Remind the children about their responsibility to keep themselves safe from all kinds of other things as well as broken glass.

Read with the children the writing on any display work they have done and seek opportunities to share this with others in the school and the wider community.

Remind the children that they have to think with their head as well as with their feelings when they have to make a decision.

First ending

'We must pick it all up,' Ian decided and bent down to pick up a jagged piece of glass and went to put it in the litter bin. Immediately his fingers touched something sharp. He looked at his hand and saw that his finger was bleeding. 'Ouch,' he said and that made Jenny look up. 'What's happened?' she said. 'Ooh, you're bleeding, go and show my mum, Ian ran over to Jenny's mum. She took one look at his finger and said, 'That must hurt, how did you do that?' Ian explained that he had put the glass into the bin and that it must have cut him. 'Mmm, we'd better clean this, I think,' she said and got out the drinking water. She poured some water over the cut and then cleaned it with a tissue. 'There, that looks better,' she said, 'But we'd better give it a good clean when we get home. I'll put this plaster on it for now, to stop the bleeding. When she had done this she went to the place where the broken glass was. 'What a mess,' she said. 'The best thing we can do is to kick it to the side here and tell the park-keeper or I'll ring the council when we get home. Don't ever pick up broken glass again, Ian,' she said. 'You should leave this for grown-ups with thick gloves on. You really weren't thinking were you? You know that glass will cut you. Oh Ian! I think we'd better take you straight home and get this cut finger seen to properly.'

Second ending

'We must pick it all up,' Ian decided and bent down to start to pick up the jagged pieces of glass. Then he thought again – suppose he cut himself on the glass. No, that probably wasn't a good idea. What should he do though? It wasn't right to leave this all here for people to fall on. He called to Jenny's mum, 'There's broken glass here, just at the end of the slide. I think we ought to move it.' 'Hang on a minute,' called Jenny's mum and she put her book down and walked over to look. 'Why,' she said, 'it looks as though someone has deliberately broken a bottle here, what a mess! No we mustn't move it, we'll cut ourselves. I'll kick it to one side and we'll tell the park-keeper on the way home. What a good job you didn't move it with your bare hands – it needs someone with tough gloves to do that.'

Ask the children to think which ending they like the best. Ask them to tell you. Can they draw or write a better one? You could help the children to make their own picture book, using their own pictures or the one from the CD-ROM.

Section I: Environment

Story 2: On the Way to School

Focus

- ▸ respect for the environment
- ▸ responsibilities in protecting the environment
- ▸ use head and feelings before making decisions
- ▸ need to protect self when making decisions.

This story is about two eight year old boys who see two older children vandalising the flowers in a park garden. At first they think it's fun and want to join in, then on thinking about it they realise that this is not the right thing to do – but just what is the right thing to do?

Either stop the story and discuss the Flag points as you read or read the story straight through and use these as discussion points before doing the activities.

Aaron and Manuel are eight years old. They had been friends for a long time, ever since Aaron had moved into the flat next door to Manuel. Every day their mothers watched from the flat balcony as the two boys walked to the junior school together.

Flag: How do you get to school? Does someone bring you? Do you come in a car or walk? Could any of you get to school with someone in your family watching you most of the way? How do people make sure you are safe when travelling to school?

It was not far to their school; through the alley, across the park and there was the school opposite them. They liked walking through the park because there were always things to see. Sometimes birds would flutter down and walk alongside the pathway in front of them. They were mostly pigeons who swayed side to side as they walked, occasionally pecking at the ground as they walked. Sometimes a pied wagtail would swoop down and make his bobbing way along the grassy verge. There were a couple of squirrels that lived in the trees nearby and they were so tame that the boys could get very near to them before the squirrels would bound away and up into the trees again. People from nearby offices ate their lunch in the park gardens and would drop crumbs for the wildlife; sometimes they would leave bits of sandwiches or pies for the birds and squirrels to eat.

Flag: Is it a good thing to feed wildlife? Could squirrels become a pest?

The path was edged with grass cut short by the council gardeners and beyond the grassy edge were flower beds. Gardeners would come and put small plants into these flower beds; the plants would grow and flower and fade. Then the gardeners would come and dig up these plants, replacing them with others for the next season. There were always some brightly coloured flowers to see and the boys sometimes noticed these as they walked to school.

Flag: Talk about the changing seasons and about how flowers have their time for flowering and setting seed.

One spring day as they were walking along they noticed some bigger boys walking among the tulips in the flower beds. They were stamping their feet and breaking all the flower heads off as they stamped. They were laughing and shouting as they spoiled flower beds and Aaron and Manuel stopped in their tracks as they saw the fun that these big boys were having. They looked at each other. 'Hey this is fun!' shouted one of the boys. The boys were enjoying themselves; it did look fun, should they join in?

Flag: Why did they want to join in? Is it because of wanting to be part of the group, being tempted or pressure from a friend to join in?

Aaron said, 'Shall we?' They knew they shouldn't really spoil the plants. Aaron and Manuel looked at each other. They ought to go; it would be time for children to go into school. They looked again at the boys. They didn't know their names, but Aaron remembered seeing one of them, the one with the red jersey, at his school in the playground. He was in Year 5 and was often in trouble at dinner time with the mid-day helpers. Aaron looked back, but he couldn't see their mums on the balcony. What would be the best thing to do?

Activities

In Circle Time, ask the children to think about the story and to think about all the different things they could do; the choices they have. Ask them to finish the sentence: 'They could…'

Make a list of the things that the children tell you. Read out the list.

They could:
- join in
- talk to the boys and be late for school
- do nothing at all, forget it
- tell their teacher at school about what had happened
- run home and tell their mums now
- tell their mums when they got home from school
- shout at the boys and tell them to stop
- run after the boys and make them stop.

Talk about the first thing that the children said about joining in. Do your children think that Aaron thought carefully before he said, 'Shall we?'

Talk with the children about making decisions and that sometimes your feelings tell you to 'do this' while your head tells you to 'think about it carefully'.

Ask the children to touch their ears if they think Aaron was deciding with his feelings.

Ask them to touch their elbows if they think he was deciding with his head.

Ask the children to work in their groups to talk about the list you have all made and to decide which they think is the best thing to do. Can they come to an agreement? Ask each group in turn to share their decision with the rest of the class. Have they all decided a sensible and safe thing to do? Could Aaron and Manuel get hurt if they do any of these things?

Have children in your class ever seen people spoiling the environment? If so, ask volunteers to tell the class about any time they saw someone doing something that would spoil the environment.

Ask children to finish the sentence: 'If I saw something like this, I would…'

Make a list of what the children say; talk about their contributions. Is it the same as the list they made for Aaron and Manuel? Ask the children to look at their list and to say which decisions are safe and which are unsafe.

Ask the children to draw what they think happened next in the story and to write about their picture. Ask them to write a list of 'do's and don'ts' to put on the back of the picture, for example, 'Do think carefully before you decide to do something,' or 'Don't stay watching and make yourself late for school'.

Ask the children to work in pairs and think of another story about someone spoiling the environment and what the watching characters in their story could do about it. Ask them to write their story and say how their person made the decision about what to do about the spoiled environment. Can some of them write two endings to their own story – one where the person made the decision with just their feelings or with just their head and a second ending where the characters made their decision about what to do using both their feelings and their head?

Ask volunteers to read their own stories to the class. Talk about the decisions the characters made and whether these were safe or unsafe. Were the decisions made with just feelings, just their head or both? You could make a wall display using the story and the children's drawings and writing. After the homework you could add some families' comments.

Homework

Ask the children to talk about this story to people at home and to ask them what they think the best decision would be. Ask them to share this with all the class at the end of Circle Time and to make a list of the families' decisions. Talk about the usefulness of these ideas and whether these decisions are safe and sensible for all the children to take.

Reflection

Remind them of the Flag points in the story.

Remind the children that they have a responsibility to keep themselves safe and that they must think of their safety before they make any decision.

Ask the children to remember that it is important for them always to think with both their head and with their feelings. Using their head and thinking how their bodies feel will help to tell them the right thing to do.

First ending

Aaron looked back, but he couldn't see their mums on the balcony. What would be the best thing to do?

The two boys looked at each other – Manuel said, 'Yes, let's,' and they were just about to join in the fun when they noticed that the park-keeper was coming to work, wheeling his bicycle along to his little hut. He saw the other boys, the ones who were vandalising the flower beds. He shouted to them to stop but they quickly ran off towards the school. When the park-keeper saw Aaron and Manuel, he stopped and called to them to ask if they knew the boys. Manuel said that he thought he had seen them before but he didn't know their names. The park-keeper said that he would be paying a visit to the school that morning to talk to the boys and their teacher about respecting the gardens. Aaron and Manuel talked about this later. They were glad that the park-keeper had come because that had stopped them from joining in.

The head teacher was disappointed to hear that two children in their school had been spoiling the environment and told the boys off. He made them write a sorry note to the park-keeper. Later that term the head teacher invited the park-keeper to come to talk to all the children about the gardens and he allowed some of the older children to help him with caring for the plants.

Second ending

Aaron looked back, but he couldn't see their mums on the balcony. What would be the best thing to do? When Aaron said, 'Shall we?' Manuel looked at him and said, 'No' straight away. He knew that it was a horrid thing to spoil the gardens and he said so. 'Come on,' he said, 'we'll be late for school. I think we ought to tell our teacher about this; they shouldn't be spoiling the gardens, the flowers are there for everyone to enjoy.'

The boys got to school just as the bell was ringing to tell everyone to go in. Aaron said, 'We shouldn't tell on those boys, they might get back at us.'

Manuel thought for a little while and then said, 'We have to tell that we saw some boys doing that, but we don't have to say who they are, anyway we don't know their names.' They did tell their teacher and she talked to the whole class about respecting the environment and how the park gardens were there for everyone to enjoy. That made Aaron feel a little ashamed that he had wanted to join in and he was so glad that they hadn't.

 Ask the children to think which ending they like the best. Ask them to tell you. Can they draw or write a better one? You could help the children to make their own picture book, using their own pictures or the one from the CD-ROM.

Section 2: Stealing

Story I: Finders Keepers

Focus

▸ respecting other people's property

▸ responsibilities when finding things

▸ use head and feelings before making decisions.

Sensitivity warning – if you have a child who is living with foster carers and think they might be upset change the setting of the story.

This story is about a six year old girl who finds a purse when she is playing on the green outside her house. She picks it up and looks inside, sees there is some money in it and thinks of all the toys she could buy.

Either stop the story and discuss the Flag points as you read or read the story straight through and use these as discussion points before doing the activities.

Janine lived with her foster family in a big old house opposite a green square. Other houses faced the green and she already knew quite a lot of the people who lived there. She hadn't lived with Auntie May and Uncle Dan for very long and she missed her old home in the middle of the town where you just opened the front door and stepped into the street. At home she hadn't been allowed to play in the street, unless she was playing with some of the older children who were neighbours. It was different in this foster house where there were three other children. It was safe to play outside on the green after school and at weekends with children from the other houses.

Flag: Do any of your children play outside their houses after school? Is it safe? Is there traffic? Are there other hazards? Talk about children who have to live with foster carers and how they might feel living away from their own homes and families.

Janine quite liked living with her foster carers; they were very kind and helped her with her school work when she got home from school. Of course she missed her mum, but it wouldn't be for very long. Auntie May was a good cook and she always gave Janine a snack when she got home from school because they didn't eat their meal until Uncle Dan came home from work at six o'clock. Sometimes her snack would be a piece of cake or a bun, sometimes an apple or orange; Janine was always hungry when she got home from school. As soon as she had finished her snack she usually went straight outside to play on the green. It was quite safe there.

One day when she went outside there were no other children playing, so she waited for them to come out. Suddenly she saw something odd in the grass and went over to look at it. It was a brown purse, not very big and not very thick. She picked it up and looked at it.

Flag: Have the children thought about the danger of picking up things they might find? Do they realise that things left about on the ground could be dangerous – especially things that have been left in public areas? (Sharp things could cut, such as knives or needles; there could be drugs such as tablets, cigarettes or things that look like sweets.) What do they think is the best thing to do if they find something that clearly should not be there?

She opened it. There was money inside – quite a lot of money to Janine. There was no name inside the purse; there were no cards. Janine looked at the money; she wasn't much good at counting up money, although they played with plastic money at school. There were two notes and some pound coins – three of them. She counted the silver ones, two of the big ones with flat sides and four of the little ones – she recognised them as 20 pence pieces. There were also a few of the copper coins.

Janine thought of all the things she could buy with this money. She didn't have many of her own toys at the foster home as most had been left at her mum's house. With this money she could buy a new doll, perhaps a Barbie; there might be enough to buy some Barbie clothes. She could buy a card to send to her mum, she could buy a bag for herself or a book. There were plenty of toys and books at the foster home, but none that really belonged to her, apart from her teddy and her three special picture books.

Flag: Has Janine already decided what to do? Has she made the decision with her head or with her feelings?

Just as she was thinking this, a door from one of the houses facing the green opened and Amran came out. He was a good friend of hers, even though he was older. He ran across to Janine and said, 'What have you got there?' She showed him the purse, opened it and they looked at the money together. 'I can buy lots of toys with this,' said Janine. Her heart was beating fast and she felt really excited inside. 'I can ask Auntie May to take me to the shop on Saturday, just think of all the things I can buy.'

'But it isn't yours!' objected Amran. 'We ought to find out who it belongs to.'

'No,' shouted Janine. 'Finder's keepers, we all know that.' Amran looked sad as he saw that it looked as though Janine meant to keep the purse. He just didn't know what to do next…

Activities

In Circle Time ask the children to think about how Janine felt when she found the purse. Ask them to show by their faces and body language how she felt and to pass this face around the circle. Ask volunteers to give you words to tell how she felt and note these down on the board.

Now ask them to think about how Amran felt when he realised that Janine meant to keep the purse. Ask the children to finish this sentence: 'I think Amran felt...' and list these words alongside the first list.

Read through the two lists. Are any of the words the same? Are they opposites?

Ask the children to close their eyes and think of all the things that Amran could say to Janine. Tell them not to tell anyone, to keep these words inside their heads and remember them. Ask them to draw a picture of Amram and Janine when she shows him the purse. Ask them to write in speech bubbles the words in their heads, what Amran could say to Janine. Explain that you will want to read out what they write to the whole group later. When all the children have finished their pictures, collect them and come back to the circle. Read out what the children have written without disclosing names. Note down any really good ideas on the board. When you have read all their work, ask the children to think about and to tell you what could happen if Amran said these things to Janine.

Talk about making decisions – what did Janine do before she said, 'Finders keepers'? Did she use her head and think about what her decision would mean or was she using her feelings and letting them run away with her?

Ask the children what could happen if Janine decided to keep the purse and spend the money. Do the children think that Janine would be right if she decided to keep the money and buy toys with it? Ask them to vote by touching their ears if they think 'finders keepers' is right. Ask them to fold their arms if they think this is stealing.

Talk with the children about the person who lost the purse. How would they feel if they never found the purse or got it back again? What would they think about the finder?

How would they feel if someone found it and returned it to them? What would they feel about the finder now? What could they do and say to show that they were glad to have it back?

30

Homework

Ask the children to take their pictures home to show to their families and to ask them what they think the best decision would be. Ask them to share their comments with all the class at the end of the next Circle Time. Does talking to their families change their mind about whether 'finders keepers' is a good rule?

Reflection

Remind them of the Flag points in the story.

Remind the children that they are in charge of what they do. They have a responsibility to think with their heads and with their feelings and only decide what to do after they have thought carefully about what could happen next. Remind them that keeping something they find is a kind of stealing. Remind them that they should give it to a grown-up who could try to find the owner.

First ending

Amran looked sad as he saw that it looked as though Janine meant to keep the purse. He just didn't know what to do next. Janine wouldn't listen to Amran and she ran indoors away from him and went up to her bedroom.

She looked at the money in the purse and thought about all the things that she could spend it on before hiding the purse behind some books on her shelf. She didn't tell anyone about it. The next day she took some of the coins from the purse and spent them on sweets on the way to school. She shared them with her friends.

As she was passing the school secretary's office that morning she overheard her telling the head teacher that old Mrs Harrison had lost her purse. She had been on the way to buy her grandson his birthday present and when she got to the shop she found her bag open and thought that her purse must have fallen out. She went all the way back home to look for it but it had gone. She went to the police but nobody had handed it in. 'Strange, that,' said the head, 'some people have no honesty have they? What a world we live in!'

Janine thought about what she had heard and felt very ashamed about what she had done. But she had spent some of the money already and couldn't hand it in now. Janine wished she could go back and change her mind about the purse but it was too late. She never, ever forgot the awful thing she had done.

Second ending

Amran looked sad as he saw that it looked as though Janine meant to keep the purse. He just didn't know what to do next. Then Janine remembered that Amran had said, 'But it isn't yours!' She stopped and looked at Amran. She thought for a little while and then she sighed. 'You're right, I suppose, it isn't mine, but I could buy some lovely things with the money.' 'No,' said Amran, 'we're going to take it to your Auntie May and tell her all about it.'

They walked along to Janine's house and went in and told Auntie May how Janine had found the purse. 'I know whose purse this is,' she said, 'It belongs to Mrs Harrison who lives four doors away from here. Let's go and take it back to her.' So Auntie May, Janine and Amran all went to Mrs Harrison's house and knocked on the door. When Mrs Harrison came to the door and they showed her the purse she cried out, 'Oh thank goodness, that's where it went. It has all my money in for buying a present for my grandson's birthday, what a good girl you are for finding it and bringing it back.' As they went back home, Auntie May said that Mrs Harrison didn't have much money and so it would mean a lot to her to have her purse returned to her. Then she said, 'I suppose you could have bought lots of things for yourself with some of that money Janine. Well, I think you need a reward for being so honest. What would you like most in the world?'

The next day, Saturday, they went to the shopping centre and Janine bought a book for herself about animals and a card with a picture on to send to her mum. She felt warm and happy inside and was so glad she hadn't kept the purse.

 Ask the children to think which ending they like the best. Ask them to tell you. Can they draw or write a better one? You could help the children to make their own picture book, using their own pictures or the one from the CD-ROM.

Section 2: Stealing

Story 2: I Want It

> **Focus**
> ▶ respecting other people's property
> ▶ responsibilities when finding things
> ▶ use head and feelings before making decisions.
>
> This story is about twins Ross and Amy Parker. Ross wants to have a special toy but because they don't have much money his mother can't buy it. He goes to a birthday party and sees the toy and is tempted to take it.
>
> Either stop the story and discuss the Flag points as you read or read the story straight through and use these as discussion points before doing the activities.

Ross and Amy Parker were twins who lived with their mother in a big town and went to the red brick school at the end of their road. Their mother went to work every day in the local newspaper shop and so before school and after school the children stayed with her at the shop. Sometimes they helped to tidy things up, sometimes they would read a comic or play with one of their own games and sometimes they were allowed to play in the yard at the back of the shop.

> **Flag:** Do some of your children have parents/carers who both work? How are they cared for? Are they allowed to go with their parents/carers when they are working?

Ms Parker didn't have a lot of money, but the job at the shop was enough to buy them all the things they needed. Of course, this is very different from all the things they wanted. There was one particular toy that Ross wanted very much. It was an electronic robot that moved and could do things.

It was also very expensive. Ross had been pestering his mum for ages and she had shown him how much it cost, so he knew it was no good asking her again. Amy said he should just forget about it. 'We'll be seven soon,' she said, 'and perhaps you'll get it for your birthday.' But Ross knew that he wouldn't – it just cost too much.

> **Flag:** Do the children know the difference between things you need and things you want? Are they sometimes the same? Are they always different? What kinds of things do children want that parents or carers cannot afford? Do children need expensive trainers, clothes with logos, things to keep up with their group?

At their school it was the custom for the children to bring just one toy to show when it was their birthday. One day at school when it was Simon's eighth birthday he brought in a robot – the very kind that Ross wanted so very much. In Circle Time he showed it to the class and told them about his party on Saturday. He gave out invitations and there was one for Ross, who was really pleased. He thought he would be able to play with the robot at the party. It sat on the teacher's shelf all day and then Simon took it home.

On Saturday, Ross's mother helped him to choose a present and card to take to the party and after lunch she had time off work to take him there. Ross went in and joined the other party children. They had a great time. After the party tea and birthday cake, they all went into Simon's bedroom to play with some of his toys. The robot was there but no-one was allowed to play with it. 'It's very special,' said Simon, 'and I don't want it broken.'

Soon it was time to go home; they put on their coats and went downstairs to be collected by their parents and carers. Then Ross remembered his bobble hat upstairs and ran back to get it. He saw the robot on the shelf, thought of the big pockets in his parka and almost before he knew what he was doing he had stretched out his hand to touch the robot...

Activities

Tell the children about something you have really wanted and yet not really needed. Tell them what you did. Ask the children to think about something they have really wanted and what they did. Did they pester their parents? Did they save up for it? Did they play with one that someone else had? Did they borrow it from someone else or did they try to 'swap'?

Talk about wanting something so badly that you might want to steal it. How does it feel when you want something so badly? Where in your body is this feeling – in your head, tummy, chest? How does it feel? What sort of things can you do to get rid of this feeling? Talk yourself out of it? Go and do something physical? Think about the things you have already got?

In the story, Ross wants this robot so badly that he is tempted to steal it. Think about his feelings as he stands there and sees the robot on the shelf. If he chooses to listen only to his feelings, he will surely put it in his pocket. If he thinks with his head he will know that he will be found out. Ask the children what they would say to Ross, can they finish the sentence: 'I would say…'

If Ross takes the robot, his twin will find out. What would Amy say to Ross if she knew he had taken the robot? Ask the children to draw a picture of the robot between Amy and Ross. Above the picture ask them to write some warnings that Amy could say if she knew he was tempted to take the robot.

Amy might say:
- ▶ What would Simon say?
- ▶ What would Mum say?
- ▶ I would have to tell on you.
- ▶ How would you feel?
- ▶ What would Simon think about you as his friend?

Collect the drawings and warnings. You could help the children to make a large class picture of the robot between the two children and paste the warnings in speech bubbles around the picture.

Ask the children to think about how they would feel if they were Simon and his best toy was stolen. Collect the words they give you and put these in a list alongside the picture under a caption suggested by the children, for example, 'Simon would feel…'

Homework

Ask the children to ask their families if any of them have been tempted to steal something. If so, how did they feel and what did they do. Ask them to ask whether anyone in their family has had anything stolen from them and if so how this made them feel. Share these comments at the next Circle Time session.

Reflection

Remind them of the Flag points in the story.

Remind the children that there will be times when they are tempted to steal something, but that their heads and how they feel will tell them the right thing to do. They have a responsibility to stop and think and should only decide what to do after they have thought carefully about what could happen next. Remind them that if they steal something, it will make them feel unhappy in the long run. They will probably be found out and then they will feel upset and angry for giving way to temptation. Remind them to think about the other person's feelings and say that if children remember that, it will make it easier to resist the temptation to steal.

First ending

He saw the robot on the shelf, thought of the big pockets in his parka and almost before he knew what he was doing he had stretched out his hand to touch the robot.

He picked it up and without thinking he stuffed it deep in his pocket. He ran downstairs and there was his mum waiting to take him home. His pocket was very full, his heart was beating loudly and he felt rather sick. 'What have I done?' he said to himself.

Once home, it was bedtime and after a bath and a story he got into bed. He said good night to Amy and to his mum and tried to get to sleep. He thought of the robot in the pocket of his parka hanging on the hook near the back door. He would like to play with it, but someone would see. He must get it upstairs so that it wouldn't give him away. Very carefully he got out of bed and crept downstairs. His mum was sitting watching the TV in the sitting room and he had to get past the door without her seeing him. His heart was in his mouth as he tiptoed by. He reached the back door and the cat woke up and began to purr. 'Shh,' he said, hoping it wouldn't make a noise and alert his mum. He put his hand in his pocket and pulled out the robot; it slipped out of his fingers and was falling, but he managed to get it with his other hand. Holding it very carefully he made his way back through the hallway and began to creep upstairs. 'Who's that?' called his mum. 'Oh crikey,' he thought, 'what can I say?' 'It's me, I've been down for a drink of water.' 'Are you OK?' she replied, not turning away from the TV. 'Yes, I'm OK, going back to bed now.' 'Right,' she said, 'I expect it's all that birthday food making you thirsty, sleep tight, love.'

He reached his bedroom and sighed thankfully – only to realise that Amy was standing at her bedroom door. 'What have you got there?' she said. 'Oh, nothing.' he said. 'Yes, you have,' she said. 'I can see it, let me look?' 'Get off!' he snapped and rushed into his bedroom concealing the robot under the covers.

Ross didn't sleep well that night and it wasn't because the robot was all hard and uncomfortable in his bed. He was beginning to realise that he had been rather bad in taking something that wasn't his. He couldn't play with it anyway because Amy would know and she would tell. His mum would be furious when she found out. 'Oh what have I done?' he said to himself.

The next morning Ross was heavy eyed as he got up from bed. He decided the only thing to do was to own up; but he knew it would be very hard. He went downstairs to his mum. 'My you look bad!' she said. 'What's up?' Ross began to cry. His mum sat him down on her knee and told him to tell her what the matter was and he didn't know quite how to start. Then Amy came rushing downstairs holding the robot. 'Look what he's got!' she said. Then Ross began to tell how he had been tempted to take Simon's robot and how he now felt bad about if because he realised that he had done something very wrong. His mum listened to him and sighed. 'Oh dear,' she said, 'what can we do about this?' Ross said, 'I'll have to take it back; will you come with me?' So that is what they did. Ross apologised to Simon and Simon's parents. The sad thing is that Simon and Ross were never quite such good friends again.

Second ending

He stretched out his hand to touch the robot, wanting to touch it and wanting to have it. He thought, 'What if I take it? No-one will know.' Then a little voice inside his head said, 'Of course people will know, you won't be able to play with it, you will be accused of stealing and Simon won't want to be your friend again.' Ross stroked the robot again and smiled sadly. 'Of course I can't steal it, that wouldn't be fair to Simon. Perhaps he'll let me play with it sometimes when it's not so new.' He picked up his bobble cap, smiled at the robot and walked calmly but sadly down the stairs to his waiting mum.

Ask the children to think which ending they like the best. Ask them to tell you. Can they draw or write a better one? You could help the children to make their own picture book, using their own pictures or the one from the CD-ROM.

Section 3: Lying

Story I: The Spoiled Painting

Focus

- why we should be truthful
- the dangers of lying
- why we need to be believed
- use head and feelings before making decisions
- where in their bodies we feel these bad feelings when telling lies.

This story is about a boy Juan who lies to prevent himself from getting into trouble. Many children lie for this reason, to escape punishment; Juan knew that he'd done something wrong and was afraid that if he answered truthfully his mother would be angry and punish him.

Either stop the story and discuss the Flag points as you read or read the story straight through and use these as discussion points before doing the activities.

Juan was nearly five years old and he lived with his mother and brother in a flat in the middle of town. His brother Manolo was much older than Juan and he was very kind and helpful. He often had to look after Juan when their mother went out and he would play games with him or read him stories. Their mother was a painter and used the small room upstairs as a studio. Sometimes people would come to the flat to look at the paintings and sometimes they would buy them.

Flag: Do the children have people who baby-sit them? Do they like a baby-sitter to look after them while their families go out at night? Do some of them have people who look after them during the day when parents or carers are not available?

Whenever their mother went out she would always remind them of what they should not do. It was a list of 'don'ts'. Don't answer the door, unless you are sure that you know who is there. Don't mess about in the kitchen. Don't go in the studio. This last 'don't' was because there were often unfinished paintings that were still wet; there would be paints set out ready for use; there would be brushes standing in turps or there would be buckets of water ready to mix paints or wash watercolour brushes. When their mother was painting she didn't mind if the children were there to watch her; it was only when she wasn't there that they were not supposed to go in the studio.

> **Flag:** What are the rules when they are left in charge of people who come to look after them? Do their parents or carers have a list of 'don't's'? What are these? Why do they make these rules? Is it for the safety of them, the children, the safety of the house or the comfort of the minders?

One Saturday evening when their mother had gone out to meet a painter friend for coffee the children got fed up of playing quiet games and decided to play hide and seek. All went well until Juan got fed up with always being found too soon and decided to hide in the studio. It was dark inside the studio as the curtains were closed and Juan didn't want to put the light on, so he felt his way around the studio and hid behind the door. 'Forty nine, fifty, coming ready or not!' shouted Manolo and began to look everywhere. After searching everywhere, he couldn't find Juan and eventually shouted 'OK, I give up, where are you?' Juan was jubilant, 'Here I am,' he shouted and flung open the door, only to lean against the painting on the easel and knock it over.

Manolo was aghast! 'Look what you've done,' he said. And just then they heard the downstairs door open as their mother returned.

The children quickly shut the studio door and went downstairs. They had supper and went to bed and it was not until the morning that their mother discovered the ruined painting. 'Oh,' she said, 'who's done this? Who's been in the studio and spoiled the painting?'

It was suddenly very quiet in the flat as the two children looked at each other. 'It wasn't me,' they both said at the same time. Mother looked at them both and said, 'Well one of you is lying, come on now, tell me the truth.' Juan went red and looked at his feet…

Activities

In Circle Time talk about accidents and how sometimes things go wrong when it is really no-one's fault. Ask volunteers to tell you of a time when they spoiled or broke something by accident and what happened. Ask the class to decide whether it was the person's fault or just bad luck.

Now talk about the accident with the painting. Whose fault was it? Was it just bad luck? Was it deliberate? Could it have been avoided? Can all the class agree on the answers to these questions? Make a list of their agreed answers.

Ask the children to think of themselves in the place of the children's mother. How would they feel if they had done a special painting and someone spoiled it? Ask volunteers to finish the sentence: 'I would feel…'

How would they feel if no-one would own up?

Ask the children to put themselves in the place of Juan. He knew he had done something wrong (going in the room), which led to the painting being spoiled. Why do they think that Juan didn't own up? Ask them all to finish the sentence: 'I think he didn't own up because…' Jot down their responses and make a note of the number of children who made the same response. Ask the children whether they think not owning up is the same as telling a lie. Jot down the numbers of those who say it is the same, asking some of those who say it isn't the same to justify their reasons.

> **I think he didn't own up because he:**
> - know he had done wrong (5)
> - was scared (10)
> - thought he would be punished (10)
> - knew his mum would be cross. (4)

How do the children think that Juan made the decision to say, 'It wasn't me!' Did he make it with his feelings without using his head or did he think about what he was saying and make the decision with his head? How do they think Juan felt inside when he spoiled the painting and when he didn't own up? Talk about where children feel these bad feelings – in their tummy, in their head or on their skin?

Ask the children to think of what advice they could give to Juan if they were there and to make a postcard to send to him. Give them each a postcard sized piece of card and ask them to draw on one side a picture of what they think Juan should do and on the other side ask them to draw a line down the middle, put Juan's name in the address side and write their short message on the other half. In Circle Time ask the children to read out their postcards. You could display some of these under a heading suggested by the children, such as 'Advice to those about to tell a lie'.

Homework

Ask the children to talk to people in their families about owning up to doing something wrong. Can they ask their families how they managed to tell the truth and own up even though they might get into trouble? Ask them to bring back to the next Circle Time their families' comments about this.

Reflection

Remind them of the Flag points in the story.

Ask the children to reflect on the immediate reaction of Juan to tell the lie and not own up. Explain that this is a quick way of acting when people do something wrong and the first thing that he would think of so that he wouldn't get into trouble. Remind them that it is hard to let their head take over and think of the results of what they say when they are tempted to lie but that with practice of always telling the truth and accepting people's anger it will become easier.

Remind the children that when people tell lies they feel it in their body somewhere – their body is telling them that this is wrong. If they can remember this feeling, it will help to tell them when they are going wrong. Remind them that though telling a lie might seem to get them out of trouble at the time, people who tell lies are usually found out and then no-one ever believes what they say even when they are telling the truth.

First ending

Juan went red and looked at his feet… He thought his mother knew it was him but didn't know what to say. He knew his mother would be really angry because he had done two bad things, the first was going into the studio when he had been told not to and the second was lying about it. How could he get out of this mess he had got himself into?

Juan looked at his brother. Manolo looked back at him, raised his eyebrows and nodded. Juan took a deep breath and said, 'I'm sorry Mum, it was me, you see it was like this…' and he explained about the hide and seek game and how it happened.

His mother looked really cross. Then she looked at Juan's tearful face and said, 'Oh well, at least you owned up.' 'I am really sorry, Mum,' Juan said. 'I really won't do it again, I promise.' Mum said, 'The worst thing was telling a lie about it, so I'm glad you thought again and told the truth. ''It has made such a mess, but perhaps I can rework some of the painting to make it alright again. You can come and help me to tidy up around the painting and help me to get started on clearing up some of the mess.'

Second ending

Juan went red and looked at his feet… He felt really bad inside, but he didn't know what to say. 'I didn't, I didn't,' he shouted. 'It wasn't me.'

'Oh Juan!' said his mum. 'You're only making it worse by telling lies. Look at your shirt – paint on it, it must have been you. Come on, tell me what happened. Telling lies about it only makes it worse.'

Then Juan's red face exploded into angry tears and he tried to blame Manolo for making him go into the studio. Manolo looked at him sadly and Mum said, 'It's no good blaming someone else Juan, if you have done something wrong you must be strong, own up to it and take your punishment.' At this, Juan sobbed some more. 'What punishment?' he thought.

Mum took Juan into the sitting room and they sat down on the sofa. 'Now Juan,' said Mum, 'Let's have the real story.' Slowly, among many tears, Juan confessed. Mum dried his tears and said, 'Well thank goodness for that. I didn't think a ghost had come in and done the damage.' What can we do to make it better?' She continued, 'You know, Juan, the bad thing was going into the studio in the first place, but even worse was telling lies about it and then trying to blame Manolo. What punishment do you think you deserve?' 'I'll be really good all day and help you to clear up the mess,' Juan said. 'I'll do without pocket money this week and set the table for tea every day without you asking me.' 'That'll do,' smiled his mum. 'Cheer up, but remember, people who tell lies get found out sooner or later and that will make a bad thing even worse.'

Ask the children to think which ending they like the best. Ask them to tell you. Can they draw or write a better one? You could help the children to make their own picture book, using their own pictures or the one from the CD-ROM.

Section 3: Lying

Story 2: The Swimming Costume

 Focus

- ▸ why we should be truthful

- ▸ the dangers of lying

- ▸ why we need to be believed

- ▸ use head and feelings before making decisions

- ▸ where in their bodies they have bad feelings when telling lies.

This story is about Alice who was jealous when she saw her friend Luce's beautiful new swimming costume and hid it. Everyone was asked if they knew where it was and Alice thought a good way out would be to lie about it.

Either stop the story and discuss the Flag points as you read or read the story straight through and use these as discussion points before doing the activities.

Alice was the oldest child in her family. She was seven years old and had three little sisters, May and Freda who were five and three and the baby Jill who was only one year old. Their mother was a classroom assistant at the local junior school and so she took Alice and May to school every morning in the car, dropping off Freda and the baby at the child minder's house on the way.

With four little girls in the family, their mother relied on Alice to help with the younger children. In the mornings Dad got up first; he went out to work very early and had his breakfast before the younger children got up. He had to make sandwiches for his lunch the night before so that he was quick in the mornings. Alice and Mum got up next and Alice got the breakfast things on the table while Mum got the baby washed and dressed with a clean nappy. Then Alice helped Freda to get dressed and they all had breakfast together at the kitchen table.

Flag: Do the children in your class help at home? Do some have regular jobs? Do they help younger siblings? How do they feel about this? Do they get pocket money for helping?

Alice was very happy to help and she loved her three little sisters, but it did mean that mornings were very busy and hectic times. As well as helping her sisters she had to remember her own things for school; putting her reading book and homework into her bag and collecting her lunch box before making sure that May had her things.

The secondary school in their area had a swimming pool. In the summer the juniors were allowed to go there and learn to swim. Their school could go every morning for one hour for the whole of the summer term, so the children in her class could have three week's swimming practice. That meant that every morning for the next three weeks she had to remember to get her swimming things ready and put them in her bag in the car.

Flag: How many of your children go swimming? How many can already swim? Do they know that it is important to be able to swim so that they will always be safe near water? How many are having swimming lessons? Ask for a show of hands of those who go swimming, have lessons or can swim a length.

Alice loved swimming, but she was a bit ashamed of her old swimming costume. She had grown a lot since she first had it and it was beginning to feel a bit tight. Alice went to have lessons at the local swimming pool; it was exciting and different going swimming with the school every morning.

Flag: Do the children realise that when we talk about 'growing out of clothes' it is not the clothes that shrink, but our bodies that are growing? Can the children give examples of how their bodies have grown over the last year?

On the third day of the first week when Alice arrived at school one of her best friends said she had got a new swimming costume and took it out of her bag to show everyone. It was lovely; blue with fishes all over it with a 'Speedo' logo on the top. Alice felt really angry that Luce had this lovely costume. Her tummy began to hurt and she began to feel hot and jealous. When everyone was sitting down for registration Alice saw this lovely costume peeping out from Luce's towel and, without thinking and when no-one was looking, she pulled it out and pushed it over into the book corner where no-one could see it.

> **Flag:** Talk about feelings of being sad or angry when other people have things you want. Explain that many people have these kinds of feelings and it's OK to feel like this as long as we don't let the feelings make us do something we know is wrong.

After registration the children lined up in the classroom ready to walk over to the secondary school. As she was waiting in the line Luce looked in her bag and pulled open the towel to see her new costume. It wasn't there. She got out of the line and emptied her bag onto a table. She picked up the towel, her hairbrush and her swimming cap, but couldn't find her costume. She shook out the towel and searched again in her bag but it wasn't anywhere there. 'Miss,' she shouted out, 'Someone's taken my swimming costume.' Miss Crowther came alongside the line and took the bag from Luce. She looked in the bag, saw that it was empty and glanced at the towel, the hairbrush and the swimming cap on the table. 'Are you sure you put it in your bag this morning?' she asked. 'Yes, yes! It's my new one, I showed it to everyone,' she shouted angrily. 'Someone must have taken it. Who's got it?' She glared around the classroom at everyone.

'Well, listen everyone,' said Miss Crowther, 'will you all please look in your bags to make sure you haven't got Luce's costume.' Everyone did so, but no-one had it. 'Oh dear,' said the teacher, 'We can't look for it now, we'll have to go or we'll all miss our swimming. Luce, you can choose either to stay at our school and go to the library with the librarian or come with us and watch from the viewing area – which would you like to do? Oh come on everyone, does anyone know where Luce's costume is? Own up or she'll have to miss her swimming and that's not fair at all. Do you know where it is?' She looked at all the children one by one, who all said, 'No Miss Crowther.' Then it was Alice's turn, she stood quietly in the line. What could she say?

She couldn't own up now – or could she?

Activities

Ask the children to think about Alice's feelings when she saw Luce's lovely swimming costume.

Ask them to finish the sentence: 'I think Alice would be feeling...' Jot down these feelings.

> **I think Alice would be feeling:**
>
> - jealous
> - envious
> - she wanted one
> - angry
>
> - unhappy
> - mad
> - fed up

Talk about feelings making us do things that we know are wrong. Alice's feelings of jealousy made her push the costume over into the book corner. Now she is faced with the problem of whether to lie about it or whether to own up and confess what she did. What do the children think that Alice will say to Miss Crowther? Ask them to finish the sentence: 'I think Alice will say...'

Ask the children to think of times when they have had these jealous feelings. Explain that we all have these kinds feelings at times – when people have things we would like. Talk about how these feelings show themselves in your body and ask them where they feel these feelings. Ask volunteers to finish the sentence: 'When I have bad feelings, I feel them in my...'

Talk about what we can do when we feel like this. If we aren't in charge of our feelings they can make us angry and do something really bad, but if we stop and think for a minute our feelings can help us to know the best thing to do. Ask the children to put themselves in Luce's place – she was feeling really good about her new costume – would it have helped if she had seen how Alice and other children who have old costumes were feeling? Could she have been less proud of her new one and not shown it off quite so much?

Now ask the children to think about Alice's feelings. She had let her feelings take control when she pushed the new costume over into the book corner, so how would she be feeling when she had had time to think about what she had done? Ask the children to draw a line down the middle of a piece of paper and to draw two pictures, one of Luce showing how she felt when her new costume had disappeared and the other a picture of Alice after she had thrown the costume into the book corner. Ask the children to write the children's feelings words around the two pictures and to write a few sentences under their pictures about how the two children felt.

At the end of the story Alice is faced with a problem. Ask volunteers to say what they think Alice is going to say to Miss Crowther. How will she get out of the mess she has got herself into? What can she do? Will she tell a lie or will she own up?

Homework

Ask the children to talk to their families about telling lies. Ask them to talk about whether there are times when it is a good idea to tell a lie; talk about these occasions during the following Circle Time. Ask the children to give suggestions of when it is kind to tell a 'white' lie, for example, when someone asks them if they think they look good with their new trousers.

Reflection

Remind them of the Flag points in the story.

Remind the children about the need to be in control of their feelings and not to let their feelings make them do things that are wrong or could hurt other people. Remind them that it takes take time to make decisions, especially important ones and that when grown-ups have important decisions to make they usually make sure that they have a good think about it. It is important to think of the outcomes of actions and think, 'If I say this, what could happen?' or 'If I do this, what could happen?' Remind them that telling a lie can seem to be a good way to get you out of immediate trouble but that people who tell lies usually get found out. People soon begin to know who tells lies and then nobody believes anything they say.

First ending

Then it was Alice's turn, she stood quietly in the line. What could she say? She couldn't own up now – or could she? Before she had time to think about the outcome of her action she found herself saying, 'No Miss Crowther,' and the teacher passed on to ask the next child. Alice began to feel hot, her face began to go red, her skin began to feel damp and uncomfortable and her tummy began to churn. What had she done? It really was a bad thing to throw the costume into the book corner, but telling a lie about it was worse. What would happen? How would Luce be able to go swimming? The enormity of what she had done made Alice feel even worse; how she wished she had not told that lie.

As Alice waited in line she heard Miss Crowther talking to Luce. 'Do you want to come with us and watch or would you rather stay in school in the library and read some books or do some drawings?'

'I think I'd rather stay and read,' she said. 'I'll go and get some books from the book corner.' Alice didn't know what to do and watched as Luce went into the book corner, heard her gasp and then shout out, 'It's here! My costume's here! I can go swimming after all.' Luce's face shone with delight as she rushed to join the queue for the bus.

'Mmm,' said Miss Crowther to herself, 'I wonder how that happened.' She saw Alice's red face and thought she had the answer.

Second ending

Then it was Alice's turn, she stood quietly in the line. What could she say? She couldn't own up now – or could she? Miss Crowther said that she would count to five and wanted the person who had removed Luce's costume to own up. 'One,' Alice felt her face getting red. 'Two,' Alice felt the churning in her tummy start. 'Three,' Alice looked around desperately to find the answer to what she could do. 'Four,' Alice gulped and said, 'It's in the book corner.' All eyes turned towards her. 'In the book corner?' queried Miss Crowther, while Luce dashed over to see. 'It's here,' she shouted. 'Oh that's great, now I can go swimming after all.'

The children lined up and started to go out to the bus, following the classroom assistant. Miss Crowther nodded to Alice to wait behind. When all the children had left the classroom Miss Crowther asked Alice to tell her how the costume managed to get itself into the book corner. Alice felt dreadful as among tears and splutters she confessed. 'I didn't mean her to miss swimming, it's just that she's always having new things and showing off about them.' Miss Crowther nodded her wise old head. 'Yes,' she said, 'sometimes it seems as though other people have everything, Alice, but you know, she has no sisters like you have, just a mum and dad at home.' Alice nodded slowly. She hadn't thought about that. How dreadful not to have sisters to be with at home. 'I'm really sorry Miss Crowther,' she said. 'I really will try not to be jealous again. I expect that's why she always likes to come to our house, to play with the little ones. I'll own up to her at playtime and tell her how sorry I am.' 'That will be hard,' said Miss Crowther, 'but I'm sure she will forgive you – you really are the best of friends, aren't you?'

Alice did tell Luce that she was really sorry; Luce forgave her, of course and they are still the best of friends.

Ask the children to think which ending they like the best. Ask them to tell you. Can they draw or write a better one? You could help the children to make their own picture book, using their own pictures or the one from the CD-ROM.

No Diving
No Running
No Pushing
No Kissing

1m

Section 4: Social Behaviours

Story I: George the First

Focus

▶ taking turns

▶ waiting in line

▶ thinking of feelings of other children

▶ use head and feelings to make the correct decision for you.

This story is about George who, even though he was only four, always wanted to be first.

Either stop the story and discuss the Flag points as you read or read the story straight through and use these as discussion points before doing the activities.

Wherever he was, George pushed to the front and never thought of waiting his turn. He was a big strong boy even though he was only four and children learned to get out of his way otherwise he would use his elbows to push them out of his way.

He was like this at school and his teacher despaired of ever getting him to wait his turn. She was always having to make him go to the end of the line if children were waiting to talk to her.

Flag: Remind the children about your rules in school about waiting your turn and not pushing into lines.

He was like this at home whenever people came to the house; he would push to the front to talk to people and interrupt their conversations.

He was like this at his horse-riding lessons, when he would push other children out of the way to mount his pony first.

He was like this at his swimming lessons in the learner pool and always had to be the first to get into the pool. Once he nearly knocked the swimming teacher into the pool! He was a good swimmer and nearly ready to move on to the big pool.

Flag: Remind the children about thinking of other people and how they would feel if a child was always interrupting or pushing.

He was like this everywhere, pushing and shoving his way to the front until the day of his fifth birthday party. It was at one of these swimming places where they have big slides that go round and round. His dad, knowing how much George always wanted to be first said, 'Come on, George – first up the big slide.' George looked at the steps that went up and up and up. He looked at the water that looked very, very deep. He looked at his friends and felt very afraid. He thought perhaps this time he would like someone else to go first. What could he say? What could he do?

Activities

Ask the children if they know children like George who always have to be first. Ask them to tell you how it makes them feel when someone pushes them out of the way. Finish the sentence: 'When people push in front of me, it makes me feel...'

When people push in front:

- I feel sad
- I feel worried
- I feel useless
- I get mad
- I want to push back
- people can get hurt
- people can get knocked over

Ask the children to think of how George felt when he gave out invitations to his birthday party at the swimming place. 'I think George would feel...'

Ask them to think of how he felt when he was encouraged to be the first to go down the very big slide. What do they think George said to his mum and the children about being first then? Ask volunteers to finish the sentence: 'I think George would say...' Collect their responses on the board and number the repeats.

Explain to the children that there could be several endings to this story. It all depends on what George said to his mum. Ask them to fold a piece of paper in half and on one half to draw George at the pool with all the other children and his mum. Ask them to write in a speech bubble what they think he would have said to his mum.

On the other half of the paper ask the children to draw and write their ending to the story.

Homework

Before the children go home tell them a little about World War Two when there was not enough food and fruit and chocolate for everyone to have what they wanted. Ask the children to talk to their families about World War Two and to find out what the government had to do to make sure the foods were shared out fairly.

Ask the children to share their findings at the next Circle Time and talk about queues and rationing. Explain that sometimes people used to try to 'queue jump' and that people in the queue would get angry and sometimes fights would break out when others tried to do this.

Reflection

Remind them of the Flag points in the story.

Remind the children about not pushing to be first, taking turns, behaving appropriately in various places and thinking of how other people could be feeling wherever they are. Remind them that George could have listened to his feelings which told him not to go on the slide, even though he was angry with himself and embarrassed for not trying. He should have used his head and told everyone that he was scared. Going up it could have been dangerous for him as he was so scared.

First ending

George gulped and looked again at the slides. 'Go on,' said one of his friends, 'You always want to be first, go first now and show us how it feels.' 'Come on, George the First,' said his dad, 'Up you go.' George looked at his dad. He really didn't want to go first this time, but he didn't know how to get out of it. He tried to get behind other children so that he wasn't at the front but everyone seemed to be looking at him.

'I'll go first,' said Tom. 'I've been here before, it's not scary; it's great fun.' So Tom went first and came whooshing down the slide, out of the covered in part and into the water with a great big splash. He came up grinning and then everyone wanted to have a go. George stayed at the very end of the line this time though and was the very last to go up. He did enjoy it and it was fun, but he stayed in line and took his turn when his birthday group went up for the second and third and even more times. George was never, ever, quite so pushy again. If he was pushy someone might remind everyone about how he held back at the slide.

Second ending

George felt like crying – here he was at his own birthday party and it was all going so very wrong. He should be the best and first and somehow he just wanted to go away and hide. The other children all rushed forward to have a turn and George couldn't bear it. While the lifeguards were supervising the rest of the birthday group, George and his dad stayed at the side watching. 'Are you scared, son?' asked his dad and George nodded silently. 'That's nothing to be ashamed of, you know,' said his dad, 'and you don't have to go on the slide if you don't want to.' He didn't. And that was that. George felt very embarrassed, especially after the swim part of the party when they were having a birthday tea. Only one of his friends said anything about George not being first and being afraid to go on the slide and he stopped when he saw how upset George was.

That night when George was in the bath, he and his mum had a long talk about it. She explained that the trouble was that he had always been so pushy and wanting to go first so everyone was surprised when he held back. He realised that this was the trouble. Anyone could say they didn't want to go on it; it was just because he had always wanted to be first that had made it worse. He resolved to try really hard to wait his turn and not push to the front in future. I wonder if he managed it?

Ask the children to think which ending they like the best. Ask them to tell you. Can they draw or write a better one? You could help the children to make their own picture book, using their own pictures or the one from the CD-ROM.

Section 4: Social Behaviours

Story 2: Sharif and his Precious Toys

Focus

▸ sharing and taking turns

▸ making and keeping friends

▸ thinking of other people's needs

▸ use head and feelings before making decisions.

This story is about Sharif who was very selfish, always wanted things for himself and would never share.

Either stop the story and discuss the Flag points as you read or read the story straight through and use these as discussion points before doing the activities.

Sharif was almost eight years old and in Year 3 at his school in the city. He didn't have any brothers or sisters at home but his parents bought him lots of toys. He liked going to school and he found the work easy. He thought he was good at everything and he seemed to have lots of friends there. At home his parents would let him ask children to come and play with him in his house but he rarely did so because he couldn't bear to share his toys with them. He was afraid that they would break them or spoil them and his toys were so very important to him.

Flag: Ask the children if they know people like this. Talk about sharing toys at home.

Of course Sharif liked to go to other people's houses to play. He didn't really like to play with them, just to play with their toys and so after a while people stopped inviting him. Then one day he realised he had very few friends at all and when his mother talked about no-one inviting him to their houses any more, he felt really uncomfortable inside and started to cry.

That night his dad, mum and he had a long talk about all this. 'Why do you think your friends won't invite you to their houses any more?' asked his dad. 'I don't know,' he replied. 'I think I do,' said his mum.

Flag: Ask the children if they can think what Mum is going to say to Sharif.

Sharif's mum said that she thought the problem was about Sharif not wanting to share his toys with other children. If he didn't want them to come to his house they wouldn't want to share their toys with him and so wouldn't invite him to their houses.

Sharif thought for a little while about this. He wanted friends, but he really didn't want to share some of his precious toys. What could he do?

Activities

Talk with the children about sharing at school. Remind them that the things in school are for all the children. Ask them if there are things they do not like to share at school and make a list. Have they said things such as 'the computer', 'some books' or 'my work'? Explain that this is normal to want some things for themselves and that if they wait their turn they will be able to have a go with everything in the end.

> **I don't like to share:**
> - a book I'm reading
> - the computer
> - a puzzle I'm doing
> - my writing
> - the magnifying glass
> - the best felt tip pens.

Talk about the precious things at school. Ask the children to tell you what the special things in your classroom are and how you take care of them. Do you have rules? Do you only let children play with them when supervised?

Talk about sharing things at home. Ask the children if they have precious toys or books that they don't want to share at home. Ask them to finish this sentence: 'I don't want to share my…because…' Explain that we all have a few very precious things that we don't want to be spoiled or broken and that it is normal to want to protect these things. Ask volunteers to say what they do to protect these special toys or things they have at home. Do they 'keep them on a high shelf', 'make sure people have clean hands', 'keep an eye on these special things' or 'only let people play with them if they themselves are there'?

Ask the children to draw themselves playing with their most precious toy or book that they have at home and to show how they are taking care of it. Ask them to write what they are doing to take care of it. You could make a display with the heading, 'We take care of these special things'.

Ask the children to think about whether things are more important than people. Ask them to raise a thumb if they think it's better to have friends than toys to play with. Ask them to touch their elbows if they think their best friend is better than their best toy. Ask children who do this to say why they feel this way.

Ask them to think about sharing friends. Remind them that their friends have other friends in other parts of their lives and that having friends can be like a spiral that can grow and spread as friends' friends can become your friends too. Ask them to draw some of their friends and to write about the things they do with these friends. Ask them to say whether these are home friends, school friends or friends from other places.

Ask the children to write their own story about someone who, at first, wouldn't share their toys and how they managed to change this behaviour.

Homework

Ask the children to talk to their families about things and friends. Ask them to try to find out whether their families have ever lost a good friend or something that they valued and which was the worst thing to lose. Ask the children to share these with the group in Circle Time and to try to decide which is most important, friends or things.

Reflection

Remind them of the Flag points in the story.

Remind the children that it is important to respect and look after their toys, books and games and that it is equally important to respect and look after their friends. Remind them that sharing toys, books and games helps to make a fair place for everyone. People who don't want to share often turn out to be lonely people with no friends.

First ending

He wanted friends, but he really didn't really want to share some of his precious toys. What could he do? Sharif listened to what his mother said and thought about it a lot. The next day he asked his mother if he could invite one of his school friends home for tea. 'But what about your toys?' said his mother. 'I think Graham would like to play with my toys and he will know that some of them are special.' Gradually Sharif invited more friends home and was pleased when they started to ask him back to their homes. He had made a good choice when he decided that taking care of toys is important but that taking care of friends is more important.

Second ending

He wanted friends, but he really didn't really want to share some of his precious toys. What could he do? Sharif listened to what his mother said and thought about it a lot. His head was telling him he ought to share his toys with his friends and to invite them home to play with him, but his feelings were also telling him that he didn't really want to share his toys with anyone. He thought about his precious train set and his collection of toy cars. What if they got broken, spoiled or stopped working because someone had not played well with them? He decided that he didn't want to share his toys with others and that he would rather just come home from school on his own and play alone. At school his teacher made sure that he shared the school toys, games and books but at home Sharif had decided not to share. He had no friends and he was often very lonely.

Ask the children to think which ending they like the best. Ask them to tell you. Can they draw or write a better one? You could help the children to make their own picture book, using their own pictures or the one from the CD-ROM.

Section 5: Justice

Story I: What About the Rules?

> **Focus**
>
> ▸ fairness of rules
>
> ▸ relevance of rules to the place and situation
>
> ▸ decisions about making and keeping rules
>
> ▸ use head and feelings before making decisions.
>
> This story is about Flora who was having difficulty in keeping to the rules in various places.
>
> Either stop the story and discuss the Flag points as you read or read the story straight through and use these as discussion points before doing the activities.

Flora was five years old and had not been at school very long. She liked playing with all the apparatus and games. She liked playing in the house and with the computer. She liked PE and playing outside at playtimes. But she didn't like keeping to the rules. When Mrs Jones said she couldn't play in the playhouse because there were already four people there she said, 'Why?' and Mrs Jones had to explain about the rule of four. When she wanted to play on the computer and Mrs Jones said she couldn't because Jamie and Harry were there, she would say, 'Why?' and Mrs Jones had to explain about the rule of two – one to play and one to watch. So you see Flora wasn't really settling in to school and its rules at all.

> **Flag:** Ask the children why they think Mrs Jones had these rules.

It was the same at home; there were rules there too. Flora's mum used to say, 'No playing in the bathroom', 'No playing in the garage' and 'No playing on the stairs'. Flora thought these were splendid places to play and she felt fed up that she wasn't allowed to play there.

Flag: Ask the children why they think Flora's mum had these rules.

One day Flora was playing with her friend Alice in Flora's bedroom. They had lots of toys out all over the place and then Alice came across a toy boat. 'We could play with this,' she said. 'Let's put some of the play people on the boats and pretend they are going for a sail.' Then she said, 'I know what, let's go in the bathroom and put some water in the bath and we can put people on the boat to give them a sail.' That sounded a good idea to Flora, until she remembered her mum's rule – 'No playing in the bathroom'. What should she do? What could she say? They could go into the bathroom – Mum was busy downstairs, she wouldn't know. What should Flora do?

Activities

Talk with the children about rules in the story. Do they think these rules are fair? Would they be able to keep these rules? What could happen if they didn't?

Ask the children to help you to make a list of your classroom rules. Talk about why these rules are in place, who made them and whether the children had a hand in deciding the classroom rules. Read out your list of rules and decide why each is in place. Are they concerned with children being safe? Are they about looking after apparatus and equipment? Are they about thinking about other people and their feelings? Draw a coloured ring around any rules that are about thinking of other people and their feelings. Ask the children to try to put these classroom rules in order of importance.

Classroom rules
- ▸ Walk carefully in the classroom.
- ▸ Keep your chair legs on the floor.
- ▸ Push your chair in when you go out.
- ▸ Wait in line for your turn.
- ▸ Don't hurt people or their feelings.
- ▸ Think about how other people feel.

Look again at the classroom rules. Are they the same as playground rules?

Make a list of the ones that are the same and add any others. Are some of the playground rules opposite to classroom rules? Ask the children to tell you why this is. Talk about different rules for different places.

Ask the children to think of two places where they go, out of school or in school. Ask them to fold a piece of paper in half and to write the names of each place at the top of each half of the paper. Ask the children to draw a picture of themselves in each of these places and write a list of rules for these two places.

Talk with the children about rules outside in the wider community, such as road safety rules and environmental rules. Who do the children think made these rules? What might happen to people who break these rules?

Library	Supermarket
▸ Talk quietly.	▸ Don't touch sweets.
▸ Don't run.	▸ Stay with Mum.
▸ Take care of books.	▸ Don't pester Mum.
▸ Borrow the right number of books.	▸ Join the queue.
	▸ Pay for things.
▸ Get books stamped.	▸ Push the trolley carefully.
▸ Bring them back on time.	

Ask the children to think of rules they would like to make about their room at home. Ask them to close their eyes and think of one rule they would make. Ask each child in the circle to finish the sentence: 'One rule I would make for my room is…' Ask volunteers what they would say to people in their family who broke this rule.

Ask the children to raise a hand if they think they have ever broken a rule. Ask them to tell you how they felt when they were breaking the rule. Where in their bodies did they feel this feeling? Was it their body telling them that they were breaking a rule that meant they were not being fair to other people or because they were doing something that was not safe?

Talk with the children about the kinds of sanctions and punishments that the government has in place for people who break the rules of the country. Do the children think these rules are fair? Who do they think made these rules? Which, if any, would the children like to change if they could?

Homework

Ask the children to draw a picture of a play park or public garden in your area. Ask them to ask someone in their family to help them to write down the name of this place and a list of the rules that they think would be sensible to have in this place. Ask them to write down what they think should happen to people who broke these rules.

Reflection

Remind them of the Flag points in the story.

Remind the children that rules are in place to make things fair and safe for everyone. Explain that if everyone keeps to the rules there will be no need for punishments, but that people who break the rules are punished because they are either not being fair to everyone else or they are doing things that are not safe for themselves or others. Explain that their body will be telling them if they know they are breaking a rule and remind them to take notice of these feelings because these feelings will help them to keep on the right track.

Remind them that breaking rules might make you feel good at the time, even though your body is telling you that you are doing wrong and that listening to your body telling you to think carefully can help you to keep rules.

First ending

Playing with water in the bath sounded a good idea to Flora, until she remembered her mum's rule – 'No playing in the bathroom'. What should she do? What could she say? They could go into the bathroom – Mum was busy downstairs, she wouldn't know. What should she do? Her tummy began that funny feeling telling her that she was thinking of doing something wrong, so she thought a bit and then said, 'I shall have to ask Mum if it's OK because we have a rule about not playing in the bathroom.' She called downstairs. 'Mum, can we play at floating the boats in the bath?' Mum thought for a moment and then said, 'Why don't you bring them downstairs and we'll fill your old baby bath in the garden and you can sail them down there.' 'That's a good idea,' said Alice, and she began to pick up the boats and play people to take them downstairs.

Second ending

Playing with water in the bath sounded a good idea to Flora, until she remembered her mum's rule – 'No playing in the bathroom'. What should she do? What could she say? They could go into the bathroom – Mum was busy downstairs, she wouldn't know. What should she do? Her tummy began that funny feeling telling her that she was thinking of doing something wrong, but she ignored it. 'Yes,' she said, 'let's do that.' So the two girls gathered up the boats and all the play people and took them into the bathroom. Flora put the plug into the bath and started the tap running. Water gushed out and began to fill the bath. They put the boats and play people into the bath and then Flora remembered her big boat that was on top of the play cupboard, so they went back into the bedroom to get it. She had to drag the chair to the cupboard and climb up to get it. Then she remembered the Lego people, so she went and searched for them. 'Come and help me,' she called to Alice and soon the girls were busy looking for more things to play with in the bath.

Meanwhile, what do you think was happening in the bathroom? Well, the water slowly rose higher and higher until it reached the overflow. Some water went into the overflow, but the water was running though the taps so quickly that it began to overflow the bath, running onto the bathroom floor and into the carpet.

When Flora and Alice got back to the bathroom the carpet was soaking and water was seeping through the floor to the ceiling downstairs. They leaned over and turned off the taps.

Flora's mother in the kitchen below felt a little drip on her arm. Then another and then another. I'm not going to tell you what happened next but I expect you can guess. Flora was a very sad little girl when she went to bed that night and thought of all the damage she had done, just because she broke the rules.

Ask the children to think which ending they like the best. Ask them to tell you. Can they draw or write a better one? You could help the children to make their own picture book, using their own pictures or the one from the CD-ROM.

Section 5: Justice

Story 2: Marc's Gang

 Focus
> ▸ fairness
>
> ▸ honesty
>
> ▸ use head and feelings before making decisions
>
> ▸ think of other people and their feelings.
>
> This story is about Marc, who was not fair to his friends when he started a gang and wanted to be the boss.
>
> Either stop the story and discuss the Flag points as you read or read the story straight through and use these as discussion points before doing the activities.

Marc had three good friends in his class and they played together very well at school. They often met up at home and played at each others' houses. Their families knew each other and all got on well together. Marc's friends were called Jason, Darren and Mansur and they were all eight years old, but Marc was almost nine.

Just before the summer holidays Mansur said it would be good if they could make themselves into a gang. Marc said that gangs were bad things and his dad wouldn't let him be in a gang but Mansur said that gangs could be good as well and he thought they could be a good gang.

 Flag: Talk to the children about gangs – are they always bad? Do they know people who are in a gang? Have they read stories about children who are in a gang?

Darren said they could call it a club, not a gang and that would make it OK. First they had to find a name for their club. They talked about this for a bit but couldn't come up with a name. Then Jason said, 'We ought to decide what the club is going to do and what it's for before we choose a name.' So they thought quite a bit about this too. Mansur said, 'We'll have to have somewhere to meet – a kind of headquarters, you know,' so they thought a bit about this until Marc said, 'And we'll have to have some rules.'

Flag: Talk with the children about how Marc and his friends were going to organise their club – have your children any suggestions to make?

The next day they went to play together after school and Marc started organising everyone. 'I'm going to be the chief,' he said, 'and you can be my men.' 'That's not fair,' said Mansur, 'why should you be the chief?' Darren said, 'I think we ought to vote on it. That would make it fairer.' 'No,' said Jason, 'I think we ought to take turns.' Marc looked at them all and frowned. This wasn't what he wanted at all. He wanted to be the chief; what could he say to make them understand? He didn't want to fall out with his buddies though. What was the best thing to do?

Activities

Remind the children about the issues raised in the Flags and talk about gangs and clubs. Ask the children to think about what they know about friendship groups or gangs from their own experience and from the books they have read. Go around the circle asking them to finish the sentence: 'I think gangs can be...'

Talk about friendship groups and about children being fair to each other. If they were going to set up a friendship group what kind of rules would they make to be fair to everyone? Ask each child to offer one rule, allowing children to 'pass' and note these rules down on the board.

> **Rules**
> - ▶ Don't be bossy.
> - ▶ Talk about things.
> - ▶ Vote to decide.
> - ▶ Share our toys.
> - ▶ Take turns to be the leader.
> - ▶ Think about how other people feel.
> - ▶ Don't keep people out.

Talk about the decision that Marc has to make and ask the children to work in pairs to find answers to the question: 'If Marc decides he wants to be the leader, what could happen?' Back in the circle ask the children to offer their responses and talk about them.

Talk about voting for the leader – which would be the best way for the children to do this? Talk about taking turns – how could they make it fair? What do the children think would be a good ending to this story? Ask them to write a good ending which would be fair to everyone and where everyone would be happy.

Talk about local and general elections when leaders for the community have to be chosen. Explain about manifestos and how these tell everyone what the person will do for the community if they are elected. Explain that these manifestos have to be true.

Organise an election for a post in your class. It could be for the school council or a post of responsibility such as care of the computer or some other item of equipment. Ask the children to draw a picture of themselves and under the picture to write what they would do as part of their job if they were elected. Ask them to write about how they would carry out their duties.

My Manifesto as book monitor

I would:

▸ take care of the books

▸ make sure they were in order

▸ take any spoilt ones to be mended

▸ display them on the open shelves

▸ help children to find books

▸ make sure they were on shelves

▸ pick up dropped books

▸ help children to take care of them.

Ask the children to think about times in the class when you have to select a leader for some activity, such as using the computer, to start off a game or to take a message. Do the children think you choose in a fair way? Can they suggest ways in which you can make it obvious to everyone that you are being fair? Ask them to work in their groups and talk about the way you make sure you treat everyone in your class in an open and fair way.

Homework

Ask the children to talk to their families about local and general elections, how these are run and how it is shown to be fair to everyone. Ask the children to find out how the candidates make themselves known to their public and about their manifesto. How do they publicise themselves – in the press, posters and letters through doors.

Reflection

Remind them of the Flag points in the story.

Remind the children that fairness comes in every aspect of life, from their playing together, life in the classroom, life at home and life outside in the wider community. Remind them that it is not enough for things to seem to be fair, it is important to make sure that fairness is seen to be fair, so that everyone is happy about it. Explain that Marc cannot just decide to be the leader; everyone has to have the chance and the choice should be fair. We are fortunate that we have a fair country with democratic elections; in some countries it is not so and people are ruled by dictators.

Remind them, too, that choices about fairness are impossible to make if you always want to have your own way. If they try to be fair to everyone they will usually find it's the best way.

First ending

Marc looked at them all and frowned. This wasn't what he wanted at all. He wanted to be the chief; what could he say to make them understand? He didn't want to fall out with his buddies though. What was the best thing to do? He suddenly felt very angry and his face went red. 'Well, I don't,' said Marc. 'I'm going to be the chief and that's that. I thought it all up and you'll have to do as I say. We'll meet tomorrow after school and sort out some rules. I'll bring a book and we can write them down.'

The next day at school Darren, Jason and Mansur got together in the playground. Jason started by saying, 'I don't like the idea of Marc being the leader. Let's not have this gang anyway; we're OK as we are.' Mansur chimed in, 'Yes, who does he think he is anyway – he's so bossy, who wants to be in his gang?' Darren said, 'Who's going to tell him?' They talked about this for a bit and then decided to go together after school and all tell Marc that they didn't like the idea and wouldn't be in a gang with him as leader.

Marc was very surprised when they told him. He was a bit angry too, but when he thought about it he realised that he had made the wrong choice. 'Darren was right,' he thought, 'We should have voted.' The four boys did become good friends again and Marc had learned a valuable lesson. Friendship was more important than being the leader of a gang.

Second ending

Marc looked at them all and frowned. This wasn't what he wanted at all. He wanted to be the chief; what could he say to make them understand? He didn't want to fall out with his buddies though. What was the best thing to do? He thought for a few minutes. 'OK,' he said, 'You're right. We ought to have an election – and there should be other leaders in the gang anyway. Why don't we all have a special job, a leader, a secretary – someone who writes things down, someone who organises the meetings and someone who decides where we shall meet?' In no time at all they had had an election and each of the boys had a special job. They decided that during the long summer holiday they would try to find ways to earn money to give to a local charity and that they would try to keep their local area clean and tidy, reporting mess and graffiti to their parents who would surely help them. It turned out to be a good gang, with them all doing sensible things in their community. I wonder if you can guess who was voted as leader? Yes, you're right, it was Marc after all.

Ask the children to think which ending they like the best. Ask them to tell you. Can they draw or write a better one? You could help the children to make their own picture book, using their own pictures or the one from the CD-ROM.

Section 6: Loss, Grief, Separation

Story I: Losing a Friend

Focus

- feelings of self when friends go away
- what you can do when friends move away
- feelings about others who move into the group
- use head and feelings before making decisions.

This story is about Alex who had a really good friend in his group at school. His friend moved away to a new house and school. Alex tries to keep in touch, but it isn't easy and then a girl comes and joins Alex's group in the classroom.

Either stop the story and discuss the Flag points as you read or read the story straight through and use these as discussion points before doing the activities.

Alex was almost six and he went to a very small infant school in the country. He had lots of friends because all the children in his class had been to the same pre-school and they knew each other really well. He had one special friend, Jon, who lived in a house near to his. They always played together, worked in the same group, sat near each other at school dinners and always managed to see each other at the weekends and holidays. Once Alex even went on holiday with Jon and his parents. So you can see that they were really good pals.

Flag: Talk about how it would feel to have one really special pal that you always played with.

One Tuesday afternoon Jon's mum rang up Alex's mum and said they would like to see them. Something had happened and they wanted to talk about it. Alex's mum said, 'Yes, of course, come round tonight after Alex has gone to bed and we'll be able to talk then.' When Jon's parents arrived, Alex's mum made some coffee and they sat in the garden room.

'Now what's all this about?' said Alex's dad. 'Don't tell me Alex has been in trouble with you or Jon.' 'No,' replied Jon's dad, 'it's nothing like that. The thing is, I've got the offer of a new job in London and we think we shall be moving and we wanted to talk to you about the boys.'

'Well that's a blow,' said Alex's mum. 'Alex will be so upset when you move; he thinks the world of your Jon. When do you go?'

'I have to start my new job right away, next Monday,' said Jon's dad. 'That means we shall be leaving this weekend, but we'll have to sell the house and so we'll be visiting sometimes at weekends until it is sold.'

The two sets of parents talked about this move and both said how much the boys would miss each other. 'Have you told Jon?' asked Alex's mum. 'No, not yet. We thought we'd tell him in the morning and I'll have to go to the school and explain that we shall be moving,' said Jon's mum.

Flag: Talk about how the two sets of parents would feel about having to tell their children that they would be separated. Ask your children how they would feel if their special friend moved away.

The next morning, over breakfast, Alex's parents told him about Jon moving to London. He couldn't believe it. He didn't want to believe it. 'That's not fair,' he shouted and stormed out of the room.

At school that morning Alex was angry. He didn't want to do his work and it was all messy and his teacher was not best pleased. At playtime he and Jon talked instead of playing and they nearly fell out of friends for the very first time. 'I don't want to go,' said Jon. 'I don't want you to go,' said Alex, 'but we can't do anything about it.'

The end of the week rushed along and soon it was Friday. 'You won't be here on Monday,' sobbed Alex. 'I'll have no-one to play with.' 'It's worse for me,' said Jon, 'I've got to go to a different school and I won't know anyone there.'

Flag: Talk to the children about which would be worse – to go to a new school on your own, or to be the one staying behind, missing your friend.

Next Monday came and Alex was quiet and sad all day. There was an empty place next to his on the table where they worked. There was an empty place next to him in the dinner hall and there was no Jon to talk to. All week Alex sat alone at his table, missing Jon. When they had to work in pairs in Circle Time, he couldn't find a partner and had to make a 'three' with two other children. He didn't want to be 'best friends' with anyone else and he was so very miserable.

The next Monday, Mrs Gale asked Sally to go and sit in the empty place next to Alex and he thought to himself. 'I'm not going to be friends with her; she can't take Jon's place.' Mrs Gale saw what was happening as Alex turned his chair away from Sally. 'Come on, Alex,' she coaxed, 'be friends with Sally and get on with your work together.' Alex thought, 'I hate this, no Jon and a girl sitting in his place. I feel all upset in my tummy and my skin is all hot. What can I do?'

Activities

Think about the choices facing Alex. He can be friendly with Sally because she's in Jon's place or he can be unfriendly. How do you think Alex is feeling?

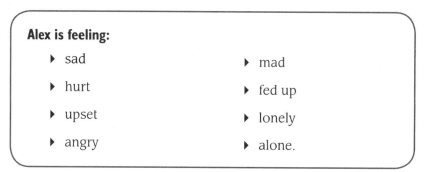

Alex is feeling:

- sad
- hurt
- upset
- angry
- mad
- fed up
- lonely
- alone.

Where do you think he feels these feelings? Think about what you would do in Alex's place. Finish the sentence: 'If I were Alex, I would...'

Ask the children to think about how Jon is feeling when he is at his new school without his best friend. Ask volunteers to give you feelings words that tell how he is feeling. Write these up on the board to make a list. Read all the words to the children and try to decide on the one that best describes Alex's feelings.

Alex wants to keep in touch with Jon. Think about the things that he can do to keep in touch. Ask the children to finish the sentence: 'Alex can keep in touch with Jon by...' Make a list of these ways and talk about the reality of using these ways of keeping in touch. Will they cost Alex money? Will he need a computer? Will Jon be able to reply at once? Ask the children to decide the best ways for them to keep in touch.

Alex can:

- make a friend with another child at school
- be glad that he has lots of other friends
- get involved in some sport
- join a new club or group
- play with his toys
- start a new hobby
- learn a skill.

Ask the children if they have ever been like Alex, with someone they care about very much going away and leaving them behind. Explain that there is nothing Alex can do about that. He can feel all these feelings, but he will have to try to get used to the idea and get on with things. Ask the volunteers to tell you some of the things that Alex can do so that he will stop missing Jon so very much.

Use the postcard idea; a postcard sized piece of card with a line drawn down the middle on one side. Ask the children to make a postcard to send to Alex, telling them what he can do to stop feeling so sad at missing Jon. Help them to write Alex's address and a short message on the lined side and a picture on the other. You could display these – some with the picture side and others with the writing side. Make a caption that reads 'Postcards for Alex.'

Ask the children to draw and write their own story about someone whose friend has to go away and how the person left behind feels. Can they write a good ending to their story?

Homework

Ask the children to talk with their families about what they do when they miss people who have gone away. Ask them to find out what they do to stay in touch and also what they do to make themselves not feel so bad at missing the person who has gone away. Ask them to share these ideas with the class at the next Circle Time.

Reflection

Remind them of the Flag points in the story.

Remind the children that Alex had a difficult decision to make. He had to decide whether to be friendly to other children in the class, particularly the girl Sally who was sitting next to him in his group. If he decides to be friendly towards her, he will probably begin to feel a little better and be able to get over losing his best friend. If he decides not to be friendly to Sally he is going to keep these unhappy feelings inside him for a long time. Remind them that it is very hard to say goodbye to friends when they have to move on and you miss them so but that being friendly to everyone can make you feel better inside too.

First ending

Alex thought, 'I hate this, no Jon and a girl sitting in his place. I feel all upset in my tummy and I feel so bad tempered. What can I do?' He looked at Sally and saw that she looked upset too. 'What's the matter?' he said. 'I don't really want to sit here in this group and leave my other group,' she said, 'and you don't want me here.' Alex thought for a moment and made up his mind. 'I don't mind you sitting in this place,' he said, 'It's where Jon used to sit, you know, and I miss him a lot. I'll try to cheer you up about leaving your group behind if you try to cheer me up about missing Jon,' he said smiling at Sally. 'I know,' said Sally. 'Why don't we both write a joint letter to Jon to say how much we are all missing him?' Alex thought that was a good idea and began to think that perhaps Sally was OK after all. It was still a bit hard for Alex at first, but after a few days Sally and Alex became friends. Not quite as good friends as Alex and Jon had been, but then that had been a rather special kind of friendship.

Second ending

Alex thought, 'I hate this, no Jon and a girl sitting in his place. I feel all upset in my tummy and my skin is all hot. What can I do?' He turned away from her and tried to get on with his work. He still felt bad inside. 'But who wants to be friends with her,' he thought, 'It's Jon I want.' This went on for a couple of days, with Alex feeling all bad inside and not doing good work at all. Mrs Gale asked his mum to come into school to talk about Alex.

That night Alex wrote an email to Jon saying how much he missed him. His mum helped him to send it and then when Alex was in the bath his mum talked to him about Jon moving. 'I know you're sad about it, really sad, but there isn't anything we can do about it,' she said. 'I think you'd feel a lot better if you started being more friendly to the children in your group, especially Sally who must feel odd being in a group where all the other children are boys.' Alex hadn't thought about that. 'I will try,' he said, 'but I do miss Jon so very much.'

That night when he was in bed Alex thought about Jon – he must be feeling a bit like Sally – all alone in a strange group. He wondered if the children at Jon's school were being friendly to him. He hoped they were – and then he thought about Sally. He hadn't been very friendly to her turning his chair away from her and not really talking to her. Before he went to sleep he began to think of what he could say to her the next morning. 'Something to cheer her up,' he thought. Perhaps he'd take his new coloured pencils to school and share them with her…

Ask the children to think which ending they like the best. Ask them to tell you. Can they draw or write a better one? You could help the children to make their own picture book, using their own pictures or the one from the CD-ROM.

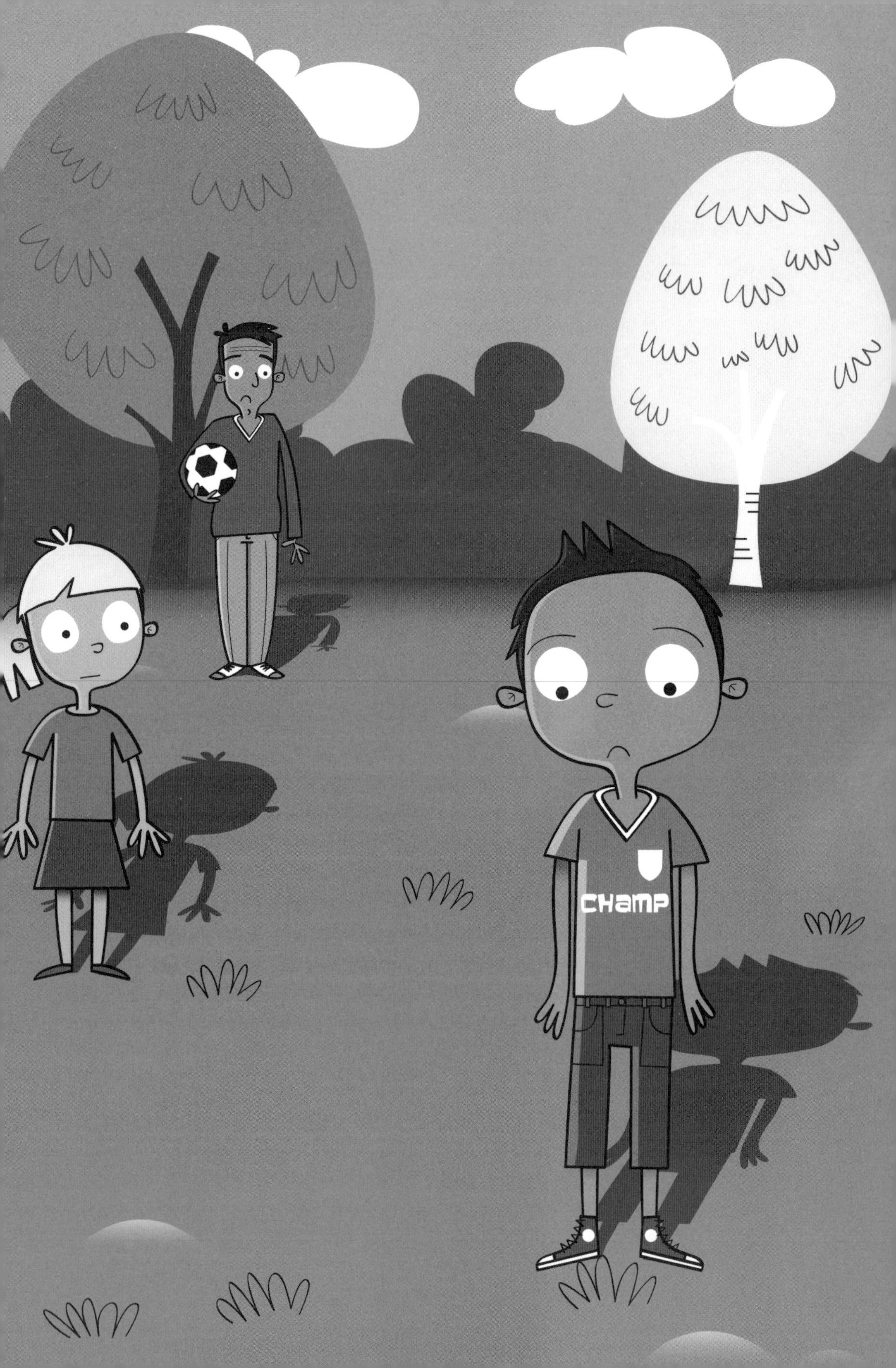
CHAMP

Section 6: Loss, Grief, Separation

Story 2: Azif and his Dad

 Focus

- ▸ missing a parent or carer through separation
- ▸ feeling sad
- ▸ use head and feelings before making decisions.

This story is about Azif and his sister; their Dad moved out so they lived with their mum and didn't see much of him. Azif not only misses his dad, he also misses his football.

Either stop the story and discuss the Flag points as you read or read the story straight through and use these as discussion points before doing the activities.

Azif lived in the town with his mum and his little sister. His dad used to live there too but his dad and mum split up and so his dad moved out to a small flat right in the middle of the town. The two children stayed with their dad every other weekend. So, after school every other Friday night Azif and his sister would pack their suitcases to go and stay with their dad until Sunday night.

 Flag: Explain what 'every other weekend' and 'every other Friday night' mean.

Sometimes they would take their cases to school and pre-school and their dad would collect them after school so they could go straight to his flat. Sometimes their dad would have to work or go away for his work and then they stayed at home and they wouldn't see Dad at all.

 Flag: Talk about parents who separate and that it is always because they don't want to stay together and it is never the fault of the children. Explain that usually both the parents want to keep the children and they have to think of what is the best for the children.

Azif was quite a big boy for seven, but his sister Jaya was rather small for her age; she was only four years old. When their dad had been at home he used to take Azif to football practice at the big secondary school every Saturday morning and sometimes Azif would be chosen to play in the Sunday match. But since their dad had moved out, Azif only went to football occasionally, sometimes every other week when his mum would take him. He hadn't been chosen for the football team once since his dad moved out.

Azif and Jaya used to play well together, sometimes in his room and sometimes in hers. They talked about how things were now and how it had been before. They both wished that their dad would come back and they could be a family again.

Flag: Talk about children wishing that parents would get together again. Explain that there is nothing that children can do about parents who decide to split up and getting them back together is not something that is in their power to do. All they can do is to love both parents and hope they can see each of them often.

One Saturday when Dad came to collect the children from the house, he told their mum that his firm was closing down and he had to move away to their new buildings or he would be out of work. The firm he worked for had found him a flat, but it was 200 miles away and he wouldn't be able to come and collect the children each fortnight as he had done before. He said that there was room for one of the children in his flat and he would like one of the children to go and live with him. He asked their mum to think about it while he took the children for the weekend and said they could talk about it when he brought the children back. Azif and Jaya and their dad talked of nothing else that weekend. Their dad said it had to be their decision. If Azif came, he could go to the school nearby and he would find someone to look after him before and after school. If Jaya came, he would find a pre-school for her until she could go to the infant school and he would find a child minder to look after her when she wasn't at pre-school.

Flag: Explain to the children that parents usually try to make sure that children are happy about the arrangements they have to make for them. Sometimes the children can choose where they live and who they live with but not always.

On Sunday afternoon Dad took the children back to their mother's house and they all sat down to talk about the change. Mum thought that if either of them should go to live with Dad, it should be Azif because he was older; she said that Jaya was too young to get used to being with a child minder and a new pre-school. She also said that Azif must choose whether to go to live with his dad or whether to stay with her.

Azif thought about it all week. Dad had told him that he could visit his mum in the school holidays but he didn't think there was a football practice team near his new flat.

Azif thought and thought. He didn't want to make a choice, but he had to decide whether to move or stay. He wanted to be with his dad and wanted to play football, but he didn't want to leave his mum or his sister. He loved Jaya and his mum; he also loved his dad. He really wanted his dad to come back home so that everything would be good again, but he knew that wouldn't happen. What should he do?

Activities

Talk with the children about Azif's feelings. How do the children think he felt when he couldn't do his weekly football? How did he feel when his dad moved out and how did he feel when he had to decide where to live? Draw three columns on the board and head these 'No football', 'Dad moved out' and 'Where to live'. Ask volunteers to tell you how they thought he felt in each of these three situations and write these feelings words in each column. Are all the feelings the same in each column? If not how are they different?

If someone went away I would feel:

▸ sad

▸ unhappy

▸ lonely

▸ upset

▸ missing him

▸ wanting to talk to him

▸ angry that he wasn't here

▸ worried that he'd forget me.

Remind the children that Azif was already missing his dad and only saw him every other weekend. Ask the children to think about how they would feel if one of their parents or carers left home and they couldn't see them often. Ask children to finish the sentence: 'I would feel…'

Remind the children about Jaya. How would she be feeling with all these changes? What do the children think she would say to her dad, her mum, her brother? Ask the children to draw a picture of the four people in this family, to write their names under each person and a short sentence to say how each person is feeling about the changes.

Ask the children to think of a time when they lost something – a toy, a pet or a friend. Ask them to think about what they did when they lost this thing. Ask volunteers to tell you. (Did they cry? Feel bad? Try to find it? Stop thinking about it?) Ask the children to draw a picture and write a sentence or story about someone looking for something that they lost and can't find. Ask them to write about how it felt.

Ask the children to think about what they do when things go wrong and they feel bad. Ask volunteers to tell you about something that went wrong and what they did to cheer themselves up. Write down these things on the board and talk about each one. Ask the children to choose one thing that they to do make themselves feel better when things go wrong. Ask them to vote with their feet and count themselves. Note the numbers alongside your list. Look at the list and numbers and ask children to explain why they voted for their choice.

Think about Azif's choice. He really wants to stay with both his parents but this is not possible. What would the children in your class say to him? Ask volunteers to give advice to Azif and consider each piece of advice they give. Is there one thing they could say to him that could help him to make this choice?

> **Advice to Azif:**
> - think carefully
> - think about Sara
> - think about your mum
> - think about your dad
> - think about your own feelings and what you think is best for you.

Homework

Ask the children to talk to their families about Azif's problem and what he has to try to decide on. Ask them to ask their parents or carers if they have ever had to make a choice like this. If they had to make such a choice, what kinds of things helped them to decide? Ask the children to write a postcard to Azif telling him what they would do if they were him.

Reflection

Remind them of the Flag points in the story.

Remind the children that these kinds of choices are very difficult to make. Azif will have to listen to his head and listen to his feelings before he decides what to do. Remind the children that listening to their body telling them the best thing to do is often the best way to make decisions.

First ending

He really wanted his dad to come back home so that everything would be good again, but he knew that wouldn't happen. What should he do? Azif talked to his mum and talked to his dad and talked to Jaya. He didn't talk to his teacher or his friends at school because he didn't want to share his problem until he had made his choice. He felt in his heart that he wanted to go with his dad and make sure he could visit his mum and Jaya in holidays but he knew that his mum and Jaya would miss him and he didn't want to hurt them. He also knew that his dad would be missing him and Jaya if he didn't choose to go with him.

In the end he decided he would go with his dad. He had a long talk with his dad the next weekend and told him how important it was to still be in touch with Jaya and his mum. They looked at all the ways that he could keep in touch. He could phone them once a week, he could send emails; he could write letters and postcards. Azif knew that he would always keep in touch with the rest of his family when he went to live with his dad.

Second ending

He really wanted his dad to come back home so that everything would be good again, but he knew that wouldn't happen. What should he do? He thought of nothing else all week and even at school when he was supposed to be working, the question kept troubling him. What was the best thing to do? In the end he decided to stay with his mum and jaya. That way he wouldn't have to make too many changes while he was only seven. His dad said that he could always change his mind when he got older if he wanted to; his mum said they would try to arrange visits in the holidays. That seemed the best choice at the moment. But as he got older he might change his mind.

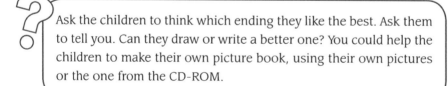

Ask the children to think which ending they like the best. Ask them to tell you. Can they draw or write a better one? You could help the children to make their own picture book, using their own pictures or the one from the CD-ROM.

Section 7: Prejudice

Story I: Suzanne's Party

 Focus

- ▸ prejudice against children who dress differently or who are not in their group
- ▸ wrong to exclude people for any reason
- ▸ use head and feelings before making decisions.

This story is about Suzanne who didn't want to invite Jacinth to her birthday party even though the rest of her group would be invited.

Either stop the story and discuss the Flag points as you read or read the story straight through and use these as discussion points before doing the activities.

Suzanne was six years old – well actually she wasn't really six yet, but she was going to have a birthday party next week and then she would be six. Her mum and dad said that she could invite five friends from school to the party. Mum said it would be a good idea to invite the children in her group at school. There would be games to play and a party tea and a birthday cake and her mum was already buying things to put into birthday bags for the children who came.

Suzanne had not been at that school for very long but she already had lots of friends in her class. There were lots of girls that she would like to invite, so it was difficult to choose who should come but she knew she didn't want to invite Jacinth! Jacinth had been at the school a long time. Her family used to live in the big house in the square but when her dad lost his job they had to sell up and move to a flat in the town. She still came to the same school but it was a long way for her to travel now.

 Flag: Ask the children to think about how Jacinth could have felt when she had to move from a big house to a small flat and travel a long way to school.

When Suzanne came home from school, her mother had bought some invitations to send and asked her to tell her the names of the girls that she wanted to come to the party. When she said that she wanted to invite the other four girls in her group, but not Jacinth, her mother put down the pen she was using to write the invitations and said, 'Why not Jacinth?' and Suzanne said she didn't like her. 'Why don't you like her?' asked her mum and Suzanne said that she was often late and in trouble, she hardly ever wore school uniform and her clothes were awful and she didn't have the right shoes. 'What do you mean the right shoes?' said her mum. 'Well,' said Suzanne, 'She wears those ugly shoes with laces. Anyway I only want my friends Hannah, Jackie, Amy and Josie; just those four, no-one else.'

Flag: Talk about the clothes the children in your class wear to school. Do they wear uniform? Do they wear the same colour cardigan or pullover? Are their skirts and trousers the same colour? Ask the children to think about whether they like school uniform and count how many say 'yes'.

Mum didn't say anything more and wrote the four children's names on the invitation cards. When her dad came home, Suzanne heard her mum talking to him about Suzanne not wanting to invite 'that girl that has just moved to live in a flat in the city centre'. 'Why doesn't she want her to come?' said Dad. 'I don't know, but we can't invite the rest of the group she sits with and not invite Jacinth. She seems a nice little girl, but Suzanne seems to have taken against her – something about her shoes.'

That night when Suzanne was in bed, her dad came to read her a story. He said he was going to tell her a story instead of reading one. It was about a little girl who had to move out of her lovely house and into a small flat because her parents couldn't afford to stay there. He asked Suzanne how she thought the little girl would be feeling if her friends didn't like her any more because she was poor. Suzanne said, 'I know you are saying this because of Jacinth, but I don't want her to come to my party.' Her dad stroked her head and talked about the different kinds of homes that children came from. He talked about children who lived in poverty and those who had a different religion to Suzanne's family and explained that these children were no different to Suzanne, just because they were poor or different in some way.

Flag: Talk about bedtimes. Ask volunteers to say if their bedtimes follow a regular pattern. Do they have a bath and a story? Do they put themselves to bed? Do they always remember to clean their teeth? Do they have a special time to go to bed?

The next morning Susanne's mother had four invitations in their envelopes all ready for her to take to school to give to her friends. 'Well,' she said, 'What about this fifth one?' Suzanne didn't know what to say. She really didn't want to invite Jacinth though…

Activities

Talk about the story of Suzanne. Remind them that we all have different home lives and different families. Remind them that some families are well off and some not so well off and that many families are in between. Ask them if they think it is right to try to keep people out of their groups because they are different.

Ask them to think about children with different hair styles, different clothes, different shoes and whether they should choose friends because of these things. Ask the children to draw a picture of Jacinth and to write about how she would feel if Suzanne excludes her from her party.

Ask the children to think about the qualities that some children have that make other children want to be their friends. What kinds of things would they look for if they went looking for a new friend? Ask them to finish the sentence: 'I would look for someone who…' List these qualities on the board and when all the children have had a turn at finishing the sentence read out the qualities and ask them to help you to put them into order of importance. Is there one quality that is more important than others?

Talk to the children about how they are all the same in so many ways and yet are all different and unique. Ask volunteers to say in which ways they are the same as each other. Make a list of their responses on the board. Ask them in which ways they are different from each other and make a second list.

Look at the two lists and see if you can pair them off, for example, we all have two eyes, but all our eyes are different. Ask the children to work in pairs and write down a list of ways in which they are different from each other. Ask each pair to draw a picture of their partner and write their partner's list alongside the drawing.

In Circle Time talk about differences between children from various regions in this country. They may speak differently, with a different accent; they may have different customs and habits because of where they live. Widen your discussion to include children of different nationalities and ask the children to tell you what they know about their language and customs.

Ask the children to touch their nose if they have ever wanted to leave someone out from a game or party. Ask volunteers to say why they wanted to do this and how it felt. Ask them to touch their ears if they have ever been left out from a game or party. Ask volunteers to tell you how they felt.

Ask the children to close their eyes and imagine someone else who was left out from a game, party or something else. It can be a girl or boy. Ask them to fold over a little flap at the bottom of a piece of paper for writing on later and on the rest of the paper to draw the picture that they made in their heads. Ask them to write in a speech bubble how the person felt when they were left out. Ask them to open up the flap and write what was happening in their picture. Ask them to write what they would say to the person who wanted them to be kept out.

Homework

Ask the children to ask people in their families if they have ever been kept out of something, such as a job, a game or a party. Ask them to say how they felt and what they did about it. Ask them if they can share this with people at school when they talk about leaving people out.

Ask them to think about how people feel if they are left out and to ask parents or carers to help them to write down a list of feelings words to take to school to share with the rest of the class.

Reflection

Remind them of the Flag points in the story.

Remind the children that it is easy to think about how they themselves feel but that as they grow older they will have to try to think of how other people feel. Suzanne had a choice to make and she would need to think of Jacinth's feelings before making this choice. Remind them that putting themselves into someone else's place and thinking of how they feel gets easier with practice.

First ending

The next morning Susanne's mother had four invitations in their envelopes all ready for her to take to school to give to her friends. 'Well,' she said, 'What about this fifth one?' Suzanne didn't know what to say. Her mouth went dry, she really didn't want to invite Jacinth though. Then she remembered what her dad had said last night – about how it would be unkind and horrid to keep someone out just because they were different in some way. She thought how Jacinth would feel if all the others in the group were there and she was left out. She made up her mind. 'OK Mum,' she said, 'Let's invite Jacinth, that would be fair.' Mum quickly wrote out the fifth invitation and put them all into Suzanne's bag. The party was a great success. Suzanne was surprised at how well Jacinth fitted in with the other girls – she kept making them laugh and everyone had a great time. After the girls went home, Mum said that Jacinth had had a good time and seemed to enjoy herself. 'Yes, she did, didn't she?' said Suzanne. 'We all got on really well together. I'm glad I invited her.'

Second ending

The next morning Susanne's mother had four invitations in their envelopes all ready for her to take to school to give to her friends. 'Well,' she said, 'What about this fifth one?' Suzanne didn't know what to say. She really didn't want to invite Jacinth though. Why should she, it was her party after all. 'No,' she said, 'I don't want to invite her; she doesn't really belong to our group.' Her mother said nothing, just put the four invitations into her bag and walked her along to school. When they got to the playground, she asked Suzanne to point out Jacinth and to Suzanne's surprise, she saw that Jacinth was playing with her four other friends. They were all playing hop-scotch on the playground markings. 'Hmm,' said Mum, 'She seems to be fitting in with Hannah, Jackie, Amy and Josie alright. I wonder if you're the one who isn't fitting in with your group.' Then it was time to go in but Suzanne kept remembering what her mother had said. She felt her mouth go cold and dry; her tummy felt all wobbly – was she the one who didn't fit in? She gave out the invitations at playtime. 'Where is Jacinth's invitation?' said Hannah. 'It won't be the same if she's not coming.' 'Yes, where is it?' said Jackie and Amy. Susanne thought quickly and made a new decision. 'Jacinth,' she said, 'I forgot to bring your invitation this morning, but I'll bring it tomorrow.' Jacinth smiled and Suzanne suddenly felt a good warm feeling all over her body. She knew this was the right thing to do. They would have a good party, all together. And they did.

Ask the children to think which ending they like the best. Ask them to tell you. Can they draw or write a better one? You could help the children to make their own picture book, using their own pictures or the one from the CD-ROM.

Section 7: Prejudice

Story 2: Arthur's Football Friends

Focus

▸ respect gender

▸ equal opportunities

▸ use head and feelings before making decisions.

This story is about Arthur who didn't want to play with girls because he thought that men and boys were better. Then he met Gina and found out the truth, that boys and girls are people and each one has personal qualities that can complement each other.

Either stop the story and discuss the Flag points as you read or read the story straight through and use these as discussion points before doing the activities.

Arthur was eight years old and had two older brothers. He lived with his dad in a small old house on the outskirts of town. His house was on a main road and so he was not allowed to play out there. At the back of the house was a hill where a lane led to a small farm. Arthur was allowed to play with his brothers along the farm lane and up in the fields, but he was not allowed to go up there on his own.

Arthur's mum had died when he was a baby. His dad had to go to work so a lady who he called Aunty Rose had looked after him until he went to school and now she helped in their house and cooked their evening meal on weekdays. She was a round motherly person and Arthur liked her very much although he felt great love for his father. 'Men are best!' he would think to himself as his dad played with him or helped him to make things.

Flag: Ask the children if they belong to families with all boys or all girls in them. Ask volunteers to say if they would like to be in a one gender family. Ask them to think about the advantages and disadvantages.

109

At school Arthur sat with a group of four other boys. Sometimes they worked well together and sometimes they played about. In the playground these five boys also played as a group and never allowed girls to join in their games. Their favourite games were ball games; handball or football. Whenever the other boys wanted to let a girl join their games Arthur would say, 'No, we don't want girls in our games, besides they're no good at football.'

One day a new girl came into their class. The teacher said that Gina would be joining their group as there was a spare chair there. She asked Arthur to look after Gina, to show her around and help her to settle in to her new school. Arthur frowned. He didn't want a girl to join his group and he certainly didn't want to have to show her around. He said, 'Can't Leroy do that, Miss? Does she have to join our group?' Mrs Robinson was cross with him and took him to one side. 'What's the matter with you today?' she said. 'Think about Gina's feelings – a new girl in a new school, of course you must help her to settle in and show her around. Just think how you would feel if you were new here.'

Flag: Ask the children what Gina could have felt when she heard that Arthur didn't want her in their group.

Then she told the children it was time for Circle Time, so they all went and made a large circle with Mrs Robinson sitting on a low chair. Miss Peters, their classroom assistant, took Gina by the hand and sat alongside her, with Arthur on her other side. They started by welcoming Gina into the circle and Mrs Robinson said, 'I want you all to say your names and something about yourself so that Gina will know something about you all.' The children were used to this and so they all said their names and finished a sentence about themselves. Then Mrs Robinson said, 'Now Gina, it's your turn.' Gina said, 'My name is Gina Oliver and I like to play football. In my last school I was in my class team and we played against other classes. I like PE and finding out about science things too.'

Arthur was aghast! A girl who liked football, oh no, he thought, and she was on his table! Well, he wasn't going to let her be in his group of five when they played. Certainly not!

Flag: Ask the children if they think there are any games that are only for boys or only for girls. Ask them to justify their answers.

Mrs Robinson smiled. 'Oh, you like football, that's good,' she said. 'You are in the right group then, because the other children in your group love to play

football. You'll all be able to play together at playtimes, won't you Arthur?'
Arthur's face fell. He certainly didn't want a girl messing up his playtimes trying to kick a ball. His heart began to beat furiously and he began to feel a bit sick in his tummy; what could he say?

Activities

Talk with the children about Arthur's family. No mum and no girls. Ask volunteers to say what kinds of things they think Arthur might have missed if there were only boys and men in his family.

Ask them to think about the kinds of things that girls would miss if there were only girls and women in their families.

Doctors and Scientists

Out of 15 girls and 14 boys:

▸ 13 girls drew female doctors.

▸ 9 girls drew female scientists.

▸ 12 boys drew male doctors.

▸ 14 boys drew male scientists.

Ask the children to fold a piece of paper in half and on one half to draw a doctor and write what the doctor is doing and on the other half to draw a scientist and write about what the scientist is doing. Tell them you don't want them to put their names on their papers this time but just to write whether they are a girl or boy. Ask the children to put their pictures in a pile to look at together in the next Circle Time. Go through each picture with the children and make a note of whether the doctors and scientists are male or female. Count up how many drew men and how many drew women. You could make a chart showing whether girls drew women and boys drew men. You could make a display of the pictures with a chart of the gender results. Talk about the results of this work and why people drew men or women. Did the children draw doctors as male if their own doctor was male?

Help the children to understand that men and women both have strengths and abilities that help them to make good doctors or good scientists.

Do a similar activity about nurses and infant teachers. Have the children fallen into the stereotype trap and drawn these as female roles? Talk about male nurses and male infant teachers. Why do the children think there are not many male teachers in infant schools?

Talk with the children about discrimination and exclusion. Explain that it is wrong to try to keep people out of groups for whatever reason. It is very wrong to make people feel that they can't belong to a group just because they are a girl or a boy.

Ask the children to write a story where the main character does something that is usually thought of as being something unusual for that gender of person, for example, a male character looking after babies or a female character being a steeplejack. Can they include in their stories a second character who is challenging the stereotyped role and someone who is justifying it?

Homework

Ask the children to talk with their families about the work that used to be traditionally men's work or women's work. Ask them to find out about how women eventually were allowed to vote and what happens in other countries about women's rights. Ask them to talk to parents and carers about the various roles of men and women. Ask them to help them to find out about the first female doctor or the first female pilot. Ask the children to draw a picture of one of these and to write about this event.

Reflection

Remind them of the Flag points in the story.

Remind the children that they are children first whether they are girls or boys and that when they grow up they can choose to do whatever kind of job they want to do. Remind them that Arthur was discriminating about girls probably because he didn't know many and there were no girls in his family. Remind the children that there used to be traditional roles for men and women but that things have now changed in this country. Men and women can do any job they like, if they have the personal qualities and the ability to carry out the job. Many men look after children while the children's mother goes to work. Explain that this is not always the case in other countries, where men and women have very traditional roles in society.

Remind them that some boys may have more strength and may be faster than some girls so they may make good footballers but some girls have agility and good ball skills that will make them good footballers too. Remind them too that if Arthur refuses to allow Gina to play with his group he is excluding her and this is a kind of bullying and very wrong.

First ending

Arthur's face fell. He certainly didn't want a girl messing up his playtimes trying to kick a ball. His heart began to beat furiously and he began to feel a bit sick in his tummy; what could he say? He looked at Mrs Robinson and saw that she was smiling. 'OK,' he said reluctantly, 'She can play, but if she's no good, she might get hurt.'

At playtime, Arthur went for the ball and kicked it to his mates who kicked it to Gina. She trapped it well, kicked it to Arthur and in no time was very much part of their practice. 'You are good,' Arthur said generously. 'Yes, we'd like you to be on our side when we play Mrs Harrison's class next week.' She was; and they came out of it the winners with 3 goals to 2. 'A really good game,' he said to Gina, 'You're one of the best! We're glad to have you on our team.'

Second ending

Arthur's face fell. He certainly didn't want a girl messing up his playtimes trying to kick a ball. His heart began to beat furiously and he began to feel a bit sick in his tummy; what could he say? 'But we don't have any girls in our team,' he said. 'We are playing Mrs Harrison's team next week and we need to practise. We don't need anyone else in our team.' Mrs Robinson's face fell and so did Gina's. 'I'll come and watch you anyway,' she said. When the day of the match came, most of the children went to watch. The two teams played well, but just after half time Arthur fell over and hurt his knee. Mrs Harrison said they could put a substitute in. Mrs Robinson looked at Gina – 'Well, what about it?' she said and Gina stepped forward. 'I can play,' she said. So that was that. The team didn't win that day, but Gina showed that she was as good as any boy and afterwards Arthur went up to her and thanked her for stepping in. 'I think you could be good for our team after all Gina,' he said, smiling at her for the first time.

 Ask the children to think which ending they like the best. Ask them to tell you. Can they draw or write a better one? You could help the children to make their own picture book, using their own pictures or the one from the CD-ROM.

Section 8: Disability

Story I: Hannah's Worries

 Focus

- ▸ eczema and skin problems
- ▸ contagious diseases
- ▸ inclusion
- ▸ use head and feelings before making decisions.

This story is about Hannah who had eczema. While eczema is not a disability, it has a disabling effect on children who have it and worry about it as well as others who may be put off by the sight of skin eruptions.

Either stop the story and discuss the Flag points as you read or read the story straight through and use these as discussion points before doing the activities.

Hannah had eczema. She had had it since being a very young child and it made the skin on her legs and inside her arms red and sore. When she started pre-school her mother talked to the teachers there about it and they were very understanding. Now she was starting the infant school Hannah was worried about it.

 Flag: Talk about the things that children worry about when they are starting a new school or going to a new place.

Poor Hannah, sometimes her skin was very, very red and itched and got really sore. The doctor had given her mother special cream to put on her skin and she had to bath or shower with a special non soapy liquid. Sometimes her skin seemed to get better and was just pink and rough. It always seemed to get worse whenever Hannah was upset or worried about things. Hannah was worried now; she always wore trousers and long sleeves to cover up the sore skin, but it showed on her wrists. But now she would have to get undressed for PE and she didn't know what she would say to the other children about her sore skin.

The first week at school wasn't too bad. They had PE outside because it was warm and sunny and they didn't really get changed, just put on their plimsolls and took off their cardigans and jerseys.

The second week was when it happened. 'PE in the hall today,' announced Ms Slater. 'Come on everyone, put on your shorts and take off your tops – just vests and shorts for hall PE, bare feet too. We shall be able to use the big apparatus.'

> **Flag:** Talk about children who do not want to get changed for PE. Ask children why this is and explain why it is important for children to have bare feet and to wear safe clothes.

Hannah felt dreadful. Her eczema had worsened these last few days and her legs were very red and sore. Her arms, too, were itchy and scaly and inside her elbows it was worse. What could she say? She just couldn't get undressed and let people see her. She would just have to say that she didn't feel well. Then they might let her go and lie down in the medical room until PE was over. 'Ms Slater,' she said, 'I don't feel well. I can't do PE, my head is hurting too much.' Ms Slater was very kind. She sent Hannah to the medical room and after the PE lesson, Hannah suddenly felt better and went back into the classroom.

> **Flag:** Talk about feelings of unhappiness that make your body feel bad in various places. What kinds of things give children these 'not well' feelings, for example, worry about dentist, worry about tests.

Two days later, though, as soon as Ms Slater said it was PE, the same thing happened. Hannah's mouth felt dry, her head ached and her skin itched so much that she could hardly keep from scratching. 'Come on, Hannah,' said Ms Slater, 'Hurry up and get ready.' What could she do this time? Should she tell Ms Slater how she felt about her skin or could she say that she wasn't well again? 'Ms Slater…' she began and then stopped. Everyone was listening. How could she tell the teacher? What could she say?

Activities

Talk to the children about eczema and how some children have these itchy red places on their skins but that they aren't 'catching'. Explain that some children with eczema also have asthma and that there are no 'cures' for these conditions but that they sometimes seem to get worse when the children are worried or unhappy about something. Ask the children to think about how their body would feel if it had red sore places on its skin and to finish the sentence: 'My body would feel...'

Ask the children to think about their feelings if they had eczema and saw people looking at their red lumpy skin. 'If I had eczema, I would feel...' Talk about these feelings.

If I had eczema I would feel:

- sad
- unhappy
- no one likes me
- don't touch it
- embarrassed
- want to hide
- want to cover my skin
- hurting inside
- self-conscious.

Ask the children to think about Hannah with her eczema. If you were Hannah's best friend what could you say to her? What could you do? Ask the children to draw a picture of Hannah with a picture of themselves showing what they could do and what they could say to Hannah to make her feel better about herself. Share these pictures in Circle Time and talk about the best ideas for making Hannah feel good about herself.

Ask the children to think of a time when they hurt their skin – perhaps by falling over, or when they knocked into something. Ask them to close their eyes and try to remember how their skin felt when it was sore and red. Ask them what kinds of things made them feel better and to finish the sentence: 'It made me feel better when...' Make a note of their responses on the board. Then ask the children to help you to make two lists from these responses under two headings – making my skin feel better, making me feel better inside. Talk about their two lists and which list was the best at making them feel better.

Ask them to draw a picture of themselves when they have hurt their skin and to write what made them feel better.

Make a display of some of these pictures and add speech bubbles about the two kinds of hurts – the actual skin hurt and the sad and unhappy feelings hurt. Use speech bubbles to show that it is just as important to mend the hurt feelings as it is to deal with the hurt skin.

Ask the children to think about Hannah again. What do they think she should do about her feelings about getting changed for PE? Should she pretend to be ill again? What else could she do? Ask volunteers to say what she might decide to do and what they think are the best things to do.

Homework

Ask the children to write a picture story about a boy who has a skin problem and say what the boy in their story did about feeling unhappy about getting changed for PE. Ask them to show their story to their families and to talk about the various things that this boy could do. Read out some of these stories in the following Circle Time and talk about them. Do the children think that a boy would be less unhappy about a skin problem than a girl? If so, why? If not, why not?

Reflection

Remind them of the Flag points in the story.

Remind the children that we are all different and special and that we all have things about our bodies that we may not be happy about – hair, height, feet. Remind them too that they can help children such as Hannah with her problem with eczema. By showing that they like her and including her in their games and thinking about how she feels they can help Hannah to forget about her skin.

Remind them, too, that it's difficult to get changed in front of people if you feel badly about your body and that it's better to talk about these things to people that you can trust and then they can help you to feel better about them.

First ending

'Ms Slater…' she began and then stopped. Everyone was listening. How could she tell the teacher? What could she say? She took a deep breath, stood up straight and looked Ms Slater in the eye. She opened her mouth and said, 'Ms Slater, I have eczema and my legs are sore, can I please keep my trousers on for PE because I feel bad about people looking at my skin.' Ms Slater looked surprised. She had not realised Hannah's problem. 'Oh my dear, poor you – I know just how you feel because I used to have eczema when I was little. What shall we do?' She thought for a little while and then said, 'Let me see,' and looked at Hannah's legs. 'We have to get changed for PE because it could be dangerous if you were wearing long trousers and they got caught up on the apparatus. Suppose you asked your mum if she could get you some longer shorts that would cover up the tops of your legs and you could wear a long sleeved close fitting tee shirt to cover your arms.' Hannah brightened up a bit. Ms Slater understood how she felt and she was helping to make her feel better. 'Just for today, keep your trousers and blouse on, and only go on the low apparatus – we'll get you all sorted out for next PE time,' she smiled. And she did.

Second ending

'Ms Slater…' she began and then stopped. Everyone was listening. How could she tell the teacher? What could she say? Hannah began to cry. 'I don't feel well,' she said. Ms Slater looked at Hannah and began to feel a bit cross. 'Come on, Hannah,' she said, 'You can't feel ill every time it's PE surely.' The classroom assistant took Hannah to the sickroom and on the way there she talked about PE and what fun it was. Hannah didn't know what to say, but when they got to the sickroom, she asked Hannah what she should write in the sick book. 'What shall I put? Shall I say Hannah doesn't like PE or Hannah feels ill at PE time?' Hannah felt worse than ever. That night after her bath, she told her mum what happened at PE time. 'You shouldn't mind what people might say,' said her mum, 'It's good for your skin to have the air on it and it will help to make the eczema better. I think I'll have to come to school and talk to Ms Slater.' That made Hannah feel even more worried! The next day Mum talked to Ms Slater in the playground. She explained about Hannah's skin and how she was very sensitive about people seeing it. 'Oh that's it, is it,' said the teacher, 'Now I understand. Leave it with me; I'll get it sorted out.'

That morning in Circle Time Ms Slater told the children all about her eczema and how she had felt unhappy at school because she didn't want children to see the red sore patches and not want to play with her. She explained about the skin condition and that it wasn't 'catching' and said that lots of children had eczema these days. 'So if you see anyone with skin that looks red and sore, you'll know what it is – and you'll want to be especially kind to them. Now has anyone here got eczema?' Gemma nodded, 'I have it on my tummy sometimes,' she said. Azif butted in, 'My sister has it all over her legs and arms, she gets upset if we say anything about it.' Ms Slater nodded and then they talked about other things. Next time at PE, Ms Slater went over to Hannah, 'OK today are we?' she smiled. Hannah smiled back – 'Yes,' she said.

Section 8: Disability

Story 2: Amjid's Secret

Focus

▸ similarities and differences

▸ diabetes isn't an illness, just a condition

▸ many people have diabetes and live a normal happy life.

This story is about Amjid who has Type 1 diabetes. He is not ill and can live a normal happy life. He does, however, have to inject himself and take care not to get hypo.

Either stop the story and discuss the Flag points as you read, or read the story straight through and use these as discussion points before doing the activities.

Amjid was already eight when he moved into the Year 3 class. He was a big strong boy, very good at football and PE. He was always friendly to the children in his class and they liked him, too, because he was fun and friendly. Amjid had a secret though and this was it. He had a condition called diabetes. None of his friends knew about this and he was afraid to tell them in case they thought he was ill or different from them and wouldn't want to play with him any more.

Amjid's diabetes meant that his body didn't make enough insulin to make the sugar in his blood give him energy to run and play. Sometimes there was too much sugar and sometimes not enough. When he was five, the doctor showed him how to inject himself with insulin and his parents checked his blood sugar level so that he was able to go to school and work and play like other children. Of course the teacher knew, but never talked about it. The only problem was hypoglycaemia (or hypo). This happens when the sugar in the blood changes and people with diabetes can start to shake, become sweaty and feel very tired or irritable. Sometimes their heart even starts pounding and all these feelings tell them that they need sugar immediately so that they will be well again. Amjid knew that if he did too much exercise just before a meal, or if he became anxious about something he could become hypo and that meant that he needed sugar quickly. That was why he always carried one or two sugary sweets just in case he began to feel ill.

Flag: Talk about your school's policy about bringing sweets or biscuits to school. What could happen to someone like Amjid if the school would not allow him to take a sugary snack to school? What would your school do if you had someone with diabetes in your class?

One day at school the teacher said that they were going on an educational visit to a farm. Amjid was really pleased about this because he had never been on a school visit before. He took the letter home to his parents and they read all the instructions. They were worried that Amjid might become too excited and then the sugar in his blood could change and he could have a hypo. 'You've got to tell your friends,' his dad said to him. 'People need to know that you have diabetes so that they can help you if you do become hypo and your friends will look out for you.'

Flag: Talk about school and class outings and how teachers have to plan everything carefully to make sure that the children are safe. What would the teacher have to do to make sure that Amjid was safe?

'No!' shouted Amjid, 'I won't, I won't tell them, I don't want everyone knowing, they'll think I'm different and sick,' and Amjid's heart began to pound as he started to become hypo. His mum gave him some sugar immediately and Amjid calmed down.

Amjid's dad thought for a little while and then said, 'Well, why not tell the classroom assistant. If you stay close to Mrs Jones and make sure that you are in her group, she would be able to watch to see that you stay well. It's clear that you can't just go off with your group of friends without someone knowing about your condition. I still think you ought to tell everyone about your diabetes, then you could stay with your own group of friends. It's your choice!'

Amjid was still angry and upset. He said, 'I don't want to stay with Mrs Jones and be in her group – they'll all think I'm a sissy if I do that! It's not fair!'

Activities

Talk to the children about diabetes and explain that children with this condition are not ill, not sick; it's just that they have to take care. Ask them if they know any other conditions like this. Explain that there are conditions, for example, autism, dyslexia and Down's syndrome, where children are not ill, just different in some ways. Talk about children who have problems with hearing or sight and some of the ways we can help them to lead a full and happy life.

Ask the children to think of what they could do to help Amjid if he were in their class. Ask those who would be worried to put up a fist. Ask those who would be sad for him to raise a thumb. Ask those who wouldn't want to play with him to touch their nose. Ask those who would want to be a buddy to him to raise two thumbs. Talk about the kinds of things friends could to for Amjid to make him feel good about himself. Make a list of the children's ideas on the board.

> **We could help Amjid if we:**
> - treat him normally
> - play with him
> - tell him jokes
> - be OK with him
> - just be his friend
> - BUT know what to do if he becomes hypo.

Talk about the word 'disabled' and ask the children to say what they think it means. Talk about Amjid who is not 'disabled' in any way, but people might say that he is. What would they say to people who called Amjid disabled? Ask the children to draw a picture of Amjid playing football and scoring a goal. Ask them to write two sentences about what Amjid needs to remember if he begins to feel strange or unwell.

Explain to the children that there is one thing they could do if they saw a child with diabetes acting strangely and looking ill, hot or very tired. They would have to tell an adult straight away because the adults in school would know exactly what to do for him. Talk about how you can tell an adult and make them listen to you. Ask the children to think about this scenario:

Two mid-day supervisors are in the playground and they are talking about something very important. A child with diabetes is looking strange and ill and another child notices and has to try and make the adults stop talking to each other and listen.

Ask the children to think about what the child can do to make the supervisory assistants stop and listen. Jot down their responses and talk about each one. Have the children realised they need to be strong and insist they are listened to? Ask them to role-play the scenario; work in fours with two being the adults, one being the child with diabetes and the other trying to interrupt the adults.

Ask the children to think about Amjid and his choices. What are the choices? Write them on the board. 'He will tell some friends and go to the farm', 'He will not tell friends and stay close to Mrs Jones.' Ask the children to close their eyes and think about how Amjid will feel if he tells his friends. Ask them to think of how Amjid will feel if he doesn't tell them and has to stay with Mrs Jones while they go off together. Ask volunteers to tell you Amjid's feelings and make two lists: 'If he tells', 'If he doesn't tell'.

Ask the children to fold a large piece of paper into four rectangular sections. In the first rectangle ask them to draw a girl called Samaya who has a medical condition that means she is different in some way. In the second, ask them to write a story about Samaya, stopping at a place where she has to make a decision about her condition. In the third rectangle ask them to write down a list of her 'feelings words' about being different and in the last rectangle ask them to write a good ending to their story.

Homework

Ask the children to talk to their families about people who have medical conditions or disabilities and who are trying to live a normal and happy life in and out of school. Ask the children to tell their families all they know about diabetes. Ask them to draw a picture of someone with diabetes and to write down all they know about the condition. Ask them to bring this work to school to share with others to make sure they've got it right.

Reflection

Remind them of the Flag points in the story.

Remind the children that there are conditions such as diabetes that are controlled with helpful drugs so that people can lead a normal and healthy life. Remind them that Amjid should tell his friends so that they could help him. Good friends would understand his problem and be able to help him in an emergency. Remind them, too, that he could keep his secret and never tell anyone, but that would mean he would miss a lot of opportunities. If he could tell everyone, explain and not make a secret of it he would enjoy a fuller and happier life.

First ending

'Well, if you want to go on the outing you've got to decide what to do, either tell the classroom assistant and stay with her or tell your group of friends so that they can look out for you. It's your choice.' Amjid was still angry and upset. He said, 'I don't want to stay with Mrs Jones and be in her group – they'll all think I'm a sissy if I do that! It's not fair!' He slammed the door as he ran into the kitchen and started sobbing. His dad came in and put his arm around Amjid's shoulders. 'Why not tell your friends, son?' he said. 'They'll understand.' 'No, no, no!' shouted Amjid. 'I'm not telling them.'

That night Amjid thought and thought about what to do. He wondered if Mrs Jones might know anyway. He really couldn't tell his friends, but perhaps it wouldn't be too bad staying with Mrs Jones...

At breakfast he was quiet. His parents didn't say anything, just waited to see what he would say, so eventually, he looked up from his porridge and said, 'I'll talk to Mrs Jones this morning and ask if I can stay with her all day. I think she might know about my diabetes and will understand.'

So that was Amjid's choice. He didn't really enjoy the outing to the farm; he wished he had been able to be with his friends. It wasn't quite the same being stuck with Mrs Jones in her group all day as he watched his friends enjoying themselves.

Second ending

'Well, if you want to go on the outing you've got to decide what to do, either tell the classroom assistant and stay with her or tell your group of friends so that they can look out for you. It's your choice.' Amjid was still angry and upset. He said, 'I don't want to stay with Mrs Jones and be in her group – they'll all think I'm a sissy if I do that! It's not fair!'

He ran from the room. 'I'm going upstairs to play on my computer,' he said as he slammed the door. Once in his bedroom he didn't know what to think. He did want to go on the trip to the farm. He had never been on a school trip before, but he didn't want his friends to know about his condition and pity him. He was used to giving himself the injections and he knew he could control his diabetes. There was really no need for his friends to know. He didn't want people thinking he was sick and strange. His mother tapped at the door. 'Can I come in?' she said. 'I want to talk to you.'

She opened the door and came inside. 'It's not the end of the world,' she said. 'Lots of people have diabetes – do you know that three people in every hundred have diabetes in the UK – that means that there will probably be one in every primary school. You're not unique; you just have to take care. It's nothing to be ashamed about, Amjid, tell your friends and then you can go be in their group on the trip.' Amjid thought about this all night. It had been his secret for so long, but...

The next morning just before Circle Time Amjid told his teacher that he wanted to tell everyone about his diabetes but he didn't know how to do it. She said, 'That's a very sensible thing to do – I've got a good idea how you can do it.' In Circle Time she started a sentence for all the class to finish: 'Something special about me is...' and when it was Amjid's turn his sentence went like this. 'Something special about me is that I have diabetes and I have to have insulin every morning so that I can live a normal life like you. The only thing is, if I get excited or tired I could become hypo, so if you see me acting strangely when we go to the farm, just tell the teacher or one of the helpers and they will look after me and make sure I eat something sugary to make me OK again.'

Ask the children to think which ending they like the best. Ask them to tell you. Can they draw or write a better one? You could help the children to make their own picture book, using their own pictures or the one from the CD-ROM.

Section 9: Risk

Story I: Julie and the Tennis Ball

> **Focus**
>
> ▸ need to identify risks
>
> ▸ need to look at all possible outcomes of actions
>
> ▸ use head and feelings before making decisions.
>
> This story is about Julie who was almost five and liked to play ball. One day she threw the ball up high and it landed in the apple tree. She tried to get it down…
>
> Either stop the story and discuss the Flag points as you read or read the story straight through and use these as discussion points before doing the activities.

Julie liked to play ball in her garden. Her older sister played tennis at the club, but Julie was not quite five and couldn't manage the tennis racquet at all, so she used to play with her sister's tennis balls in the garden, throwing them up to the wall and catching them, sometimes, or throwing them up into the air and not catching them sometimes.

One day as Julie was playing ball in the garden, she threw the ball up really high and it didn't come down. She looked up and up and couldn't see it at all. She wondered if it had gone up into the apple tree but she couldn't see it, so she looked around the garden to see what she could use to help her. There was a wrought iron garden table and four chairs on the patio nearby. Julie pulled one of the chairs a bit nearer towards the tree, climbed on it, stood and stretched up and at last she spied the ball, caught up in the branches.

> **Flag:** Ask the children to consider whether this could be risky behaviour. Do they think that Julie could hurt herself? Has she thought about this?

Julie tried to shake the tree, but it was a very old tree, solid and strong. She looked at the garden table and thought that if she dragged it nearer to the tree she might be able to reach the ball, so she dragged it underneath the lower branches and climbed on it. No way. The ball was really high up; even when she stretched up high she couldn't reach it. Then she had another idea. Suppose she put the chair on top of the table and climbed on that, then she would be able to reach it.

Flag: Ask the children what they think of this kind of behaviour. Can they think of a safer way to try to get the ball?

She pulled the chair and heaved it up onto its side on the table, then she climbed on the table again and put the chair onto its legs. It wobbled a bit as she did this and Julie began to feel a bit worried. It looked easy to climb on the chair which was on the table, but when it wobbled it made her insides go a bit wobbly too, just as if her heart jumped. Suppose the chair fell and she fell with it. Was it really safe to climb up? Julie reached for the seat of the chair to heave herself up and it wobbled again. Was this risky? Could it all fall down and would she hurt herself? What was the best thing to do?

Activities

Talk to the children about the Flag points in the story. Ask them to think of better things that Julie could do if she wants to get the ball out of the tree. Ask them to finish the sentence: 'Julie could…' Make a list on the board of the things the children tell you. When everyone has had a turn ask the children to look at the list and try to decide the very best thing that Julie could do.

Julie could:

- ask her sister to help

- ask her mum

- use a safe ladder

- throw something up to knock it down

- leave the ball there and play something else.

Ask the children if they have ever climbed up on something that was wobbly. Ask volunteers to say how it made them feel and where these feelings were. Collect these feelings and read them through with the children. Can they add any more? Make a list to display on the wall under a heading such as 'Wobbly feelings'.

Have the children ever gone across a wobbly bridge, or had to walk along a narrow plank or stepping stones over a stream? Ask the children to draw a picture and write a story about someone who wanted to get to the other side of a stream and how they felt as they were doing it. Did they take a risk? Did they make sure that it was safe? Share these pictures and stories. You could ask the children to help you to make a class book. Ask them to think of a good title for the book.

Talk to the children about their responsibility to keep themselves safe. Ask them to give you examples of other things that children might do that are risky or dangerous and talk about these. Explain to the children that sometimes risky or dangerous actions can be made safe if people take precautions by having the right equipment or wearing the right kinds of clothes. Ask them to work in pairs and think of something that a child might do that could be dangerous, but could be safe if they took sensible precautions. Ask them to fold a piece of paper into two halves and write the headings 'Unsafe' on

one half and 'Safe' on the other. Ask them to draw the action on the two pieces of paper and write a sentence about what makes the action safe in the second picture.

Homework

Ask the children to look around their homes at the high shelves or cupboards where people store things that they don't use often. How do the grown-ups in their home get things down from these high places? Ask the children to make a list of all the high places in their bedroom and to say how they get things down from these places. Is it always a safe way or do they take risks?

Reflection

Remind them of the Flag points in the story.

Remind the children that before they act they should always look ahead to see what could happen. It's never clever to climb on things that are unsafe, sometimes you might get away with it but often people fall and hurt themselves and then other people have to help out.

First ending

Julie reached for the seat of the chair to heave herself up and it wobbled again. Was this risky? Could it all fall down and would she hurt herself? What was the best thing to do? She did want the ball though and so she stretched to clamber on to the seat. It wobbled and she reached out for the tree trunk to steady herself. Then the chair began to slide along the top of the table because she was leaning towards the tree. She tried to move back but it was too late. The table wobbled, the chair slipped and Julie tumbled off onto the ground below with the table and chair on top of her. 'Mummmm!' she yelled as she tried to sit up and couldn't. Her knee was hurting so very much. It felt a bit wet. 'Help me, Mum,' she called again but nobody came. Then she heard something, it was her sister coming home from secondary school. 'Help, oh please help me,' she called and her sister came running down the garden path towards her. 'What's happened, Julie?' she called as she tried to get the heavy iron table off her little sister. Julie moaned as she scrambled out from under the table and chair. She did look a mess. Her dress was all torn and her knee was cut from side to side. There was blood everywhere. 'Oh my,' said her sister. 'I think we need a doctor to see this.' Julie tried not to cry but when she saw all the blood her face went white and she started to yell even louder.

Just then Mum came out; she had been up in the bedrooms putting away the clean clothes and when she heard Julie screaming she came running. 'Oh

Julie, what have you been up to now?' she said when she saw all the blood and Julie's tearful face. 'Right, I'll get the car out to take her to Casualty but first we'll wrap that up.' She turned to Julie's sister and told her to get an old clean towel out of the kitchen drawer and comforted Julie as they sat on the grass waiting. Soon her knee was wrapped up and they were all in the car and on the way. The doctor had to put five stitches in Julie's knee and it was some time before she could walk without pain.

Second ending

Julie reached for the seat of the chair to heave herself up and it wobbled again. Was this risky? Could it all fall down and would she hurt herself? What was the best thing to do? She started to climb on the table but as she reached towards the chair it moved and Julie realised that this was a bad choice. Suppose the whole lot fell down on top of her. The table was quite heavy but it was a bit wobbly on the uneven grass. She looked at the table and chair again; she did want the ball, but when the chair moved it made Julie's inside feel wobbly. 'Better not,' she thought. She had made her choice and that was not to climb on it. Carefully she took the chair off the table and began to drag it back to the patio. She was just moving the table back when her mum came out into the garden and saw what she was doing. 'What on earth are you doing?' she called. 'It's my ball,' said Julie, 'it's stuck up in the apple tree and I can't reach it.' 'I can see it,' said Mum. 'Well we'll just have to wait until Dad comes home and he can get the ladder and get it down for you.'

And that's what they did. It was easy for Dad, although he did ask Mum to stand at the bottom of the ladder to make sure it was steady.

Ask the children to think which ending they like the best. Ask them to tell you. Can they draw or write a better one? You could help the children to make their own picture book, using their own pictures or the one from the CD-ROM.

Section 9: Risk

Story 2: Josh and the Canal

 Focus

> ‣ need to identify risks
>
> ‣ need to look at all possible outcomes of actions
>
> ‣ use head and feelings before making decisions.
>
> This story is about Josh who wanted to play by the canal. His mother had told him he could only go there when he was with his older brother but Josh thought he would be safe with a friend.
>
> Either stop the story and discuss the Flag points as you read or read the story straight through and use these as discussion points before doing the activities.

Josh lived near a canal, well not very near, he had to go along his street and around the corner to the next street before he got to the canal. He sometimes used to go with his brother Ben to take their dog for a walk along the canal path. His mother said he must only go near the canal when he was with Ben, because she was afraid that he would fall in and even though he could swim in the swimming pool it was not the same as trying to swim in a dirty canal. So that was the rule.

 Flag: Talk about the difference between swimming in a controlled environment and swimming in a canal or river. What are the dangers? What are the risks?

Josh had lots of friends from school and several of them lived in the long street where Josh lived. They were all round about the same age as Josh – eight, coming up to nine. There was one older boy called Gavin that Josh was particularly friendly with and they used to play together after school and at weekends and in the school holidays. He lived in the next street, the one near the canal.

One day Josh was playing with his friend when Gavin said, 'Let's go to the canal and see if there are any boats or barges going down. We can play on the bridge and drop bits of wood over the edge and watch them float to the other side.' 'I can't go to the canal unless Ben's with me,' said Josh.

'Ooo!' said Gavin. 'Who's a scaredy cat then?'

'No, I'm not scared, but Mum's scared I'll fall in and says I can only go there with Ben.'

'Well, I'm going anyway, you stay behind if you're scared.'

Josh felt really bad. He wanted to go to the canal; he knew he shouldn't. But Gavin was going and if he was with his friend it was almost the same as being with Ben, wasn't it?

 Flag: Is being with your friends the same as being with a big brother?

'Wait for me, I'm coming,' he said as he ran to join him. When they got to the canal there were no barges, so they sat on the edge of the towpath with their legs dangling over. Then they saw, of all things, a pretty toy boat floating down the canal. It was red with white sails and looked almost new.

'Hey look at that!' said Gavin. 'Let's get it.'

He got a stick and leaned over the water, but couldn't get the boat.

'Look Josh,' he said, 'if you get through the bars on the bridge and stand on the edge you'll be able to get it with the stick as it comes under and I'll swish the water towards you.' Josh thought for a moment. What should he do?

Activities

Talk with the children about the Flag points and the dangers of playing near water. Ask the children what safeguards there usually are near rivers and canals. Do they know about lifelines and lifebuoys? Do they know that children should not jump in to try to save someone, but use a line, a buoy or a long stick? Talk about the risk of jumping into unknown waters. Ask them to finish the sentence: 'It's risky to jump in because...'

It's risky to jump in because:

▸ you don't know how deep it is

▸ anything could be underneath

▸ you could drown

▸ you could hurt your legs

▸ you could swallow dirty water

▸ your clothes could pull you down

▸ someone would have to save you

▸ the water could be polluted

▸ it's hard to swim with clothes on

▸ a boat could come and hurt you.

Ask them to draw Josh and Gavin at the canal. Ask them to give Gavin a large speech bubble and to write in it the words that he will say to try to try to persuade Josh to go on the bridge and through the bars. Ask them to write anything else that Gavin might say to try to persuade Josh. Talk with the children about what people say to try to persuade you to do something you don't really want to do. Remind them that they have to resist this kind of persuasion.

Ask the children to think about what they would do if they were Josh. Would they go and get through the bars of the bridge and stand on the edge? What sort of things could happen if he did that? Would he be doing something brave? Would he be doing something risky? How would he feel if Gavin calls him a wimp? Talk about the need to resist pressure such as this. Ask the children to practise saying 'No' firmly and confidently.

Ask the children to work in pairs and make up a story about someone else trying to persuade someone to do something that could be dangerous or risky. Ask them to draw a picture of the place where this is happening in their story. Ask them to write down the risks as a numbered list. Ask them to think about and to write down anything the person in their story could do to make the risks less, for example, wearing special clothing or equipment, using a phone and calling for help. Share some of these pictures and stories with the whole class and talk about other ways to lessen the risks.

Ask the children to think of a really good ending to the story of Josh and Gavin at the canal. Ask them to draw and write this really good ending where no-one gets hurt and where no-one has their feelings hurt.

Homework

Ask the children to design a safety message that can be used near rivers, canals or the sea. Ask them to make sure their message is short and clear and to write it boldly so that it could be displayed near the water. They can decorate their message with suitable icons or pictures. Display these pictures for a day on some part of the classroom wall. Ask the children to vote on the best one that acts as a warning.

Reflection

Remind them of the Flag points in the story.

Remind the children of the need to take care near water. Remind them that they must resist pressure from other people, even if they are best friends, who try to persuade them to do something that they know is dangerous, risky or wrong.

First ending

'Stand on the edge, you'll be able to get it as it comes under.' Josh thought for a moment. What should he do? He thought that Gavin would mock him if he didn't and it was a pretty little boat. Then he remembered that he shouldn't really be here. What would his mum say if she could see him now? He began to go hot and cold all over. He took a deep breath. 'Great!' he said loudly. 'You want me to go and climb through those rails on the bridge and lean over and get the boat? You're mad, it's far too risky! Come on Gavin, just leave it.'

Gavin leaned back to the bank and threw the stick into the river. 'It's too late now anyway,' he said, 'look the boat's gone.' The two boys walked back along the canal bank and turned into the street where Gavin lived.

Josh saw his mother talking to a friend. Josh's mother saw him. 'Where've you been?' she said, angrily. 'I've told you not to go near the canal, you've no sense at all.' And she took him home, grumbling all the while about how he could have been drowned and she wouldn't have known anything about it.

Second ending

'Stand on the edge you'll be able to get it as if comes under.' Josh thought for a moment. What should he do? He knew that Gavin would call him a wimp if he didn't do that, so he went to the bridge. His tummy was feeling a bit queasy and he was sweating a bit as he walked nearer to the middle and squeezed through the bars. As he looked down into the water, his head began to swim and he felt as though he was going to fall in… 'I shouldn't be doing this,' he thought; he leaned over further, tried to grab the boat, lost his footing, slipped and fell.

There was an almighty splash as Josh hit the water. Gavin went white as he saw what had happened. He ran along the path, grabbing a stick on the way. 'Here,' he shouted, 'Grab this'. Josh reached for the stick and Gavin slowly pulled him to the bank. A small crowd of people had stopped to see the drama. A man helped Gavin to get Josh up onto the bank and out of the water. 'You're lucky,' he said, 'This could have turned out much worse.'

Josh stood on the bank. Water poured off him, from his shoes, his trouser pockets and his tee shirt. He pushed back his wet hair, smiled his thanks and tried to think what to do next. 'Oh dear,' he thought, 'How am I going to get out of this mess? My mum'll half kill me when she finds out!'

Ask the children to think which ending they like the best. Ask them to tell you. Can they draw or write a better one? You could help the children to make their own picture book, using their own pictures or the one from the CD-ROM.